jams and preserves

Contents

Notes

Standard level spoon measurements are used in all recipes.

Milk should be homogenized unless otherwise stated.

Fresh herbs should be used unless otherwise stated. If unavailable, use dried herbs as an alternative but half the quantities stated.

Ovens should be pre-heated to the specified temperature—if using a convection oven, follow manufacturer's instructions for adjusting the time and the temperature.

Pepper should be freshly ground black pepper unless otherwise stated.

Preserving jars should be sterilized before use. Some fruits and vegetables need to be blanched before sterilization.

Nuts and nut derivatives:
This book includes dishes made with nuts and nut derivatives. It is advisable for readers with known allergic reactions to nuts and nut derivatives and those who may be potentially vulnerable to these allergies, such as pregnant and breastfeeding mothers, invalids, the elderly, babies and children, to avoid dishes made with nuts and nut oils. It is also prudent to check the labels of pre-prepared ingredients for the possible inclusion of nut derivatives.

Vegetarians should look for the "V" symbol on a cheese to ensure it is made with vegetarian rennet. There are vegetarian forms of Parmesan, Feta, Cheddar, Cheshire, Red Leicester, dolcelatte and many goat cheeses, among others.

jams and preserves

photography by Akiko Ida

HACHETTE
Illustrated

If you turn your garden produce into preserves, you will have the pleasure of eating healthy, natural fruits and vegetables all year round, in and out of season. Making preserves is easy. Here are all the tips you need to be successful.

It is very easy to preserve fruit and vegetables at home. Anyone—even beginners—can achieve great results, but you do need to be fussy about quality. Only really good-quality fruits and vegetables make good preserves.

If you are lucky enough to have fruit trees or a vegetable garden, the best time to pick the produce is in the early morning, before the sun gets hot, but wait until the dew has evaporated. Avoid picking fruit and vegetables in wet weather. It is best to harvest fruits and vegetables early in the season, when they are just ripe.

For successful preserves, you must follow strict food safety rules. Use only proper preserving jars, with rubber seals and metal clips or screw-tops. You can use the jars over and over again, but you must use a brand-new rubber seal each time.

There are two ways to sterilize the jars after filling: you can boil them or use a pressure-cooker.

Be careful
With certain dishes
For preserving fish, poultry or meat, and for some vegetables with a low acidity, you are strongly recommended to use a pressure cooker. A high temperature—above the normal boiling point of water at 212°F—is required to kill bacteria and to prevent the growth of molds, yeasts, etc. Obviously, this is not possible using a simple saucepan.

When preserves go bad
If the cover of a preserving jar has "blown"—that is, bulges—if it opens too easily, if the rubber seal has become distended, or if you discover mold in the jar, don't take risks. Throw the preserve away.

Sterilization
Blanching fruits and vegetables
Some fruits and vegetables need to be blanched as well as washed before they are sterilized. Blanching helps retain their colour and prevents them from becoming too acid. Don't forget to rinse fruit and vegetables after blanching. And you should never re-use the blanching water for cooking the produce.

Sterilizing jars
Before using preserving jars, you should wash and dry them. Then place them in a pan of boiling water for several minutes in order to sterilize them. Stand the jars upside down to drain on a clean kitchen towel. You may also sterilize them in your oven at 225°F for 5 minutes.

Bottling
When filling jars, do not press down on the fruit or vegetables. When adding liquid, never fill the jar completely. Leave a headspace of at least ¾ inch, so that the rubber seal does not burst or distort during sterilization.

Sealing
Once you have filled the jar, don't forget to fit a brand-new rubber seal. The seal is designed to keep air out of the jar.

Sterilizing the preserves
To minimize disturbance to the jar during sterilization, wrap it in a cloth after ensuring the seal is airtight. Place the jar in a large saucepan or pressure cooker. Add water to cover. If using a pressure cooker, reduce the time given in the recipe by one-third. If you do not have a pressure cooker, a large saucepan will do, provided it is sufficiently deep to prevent it from boiling over. Pay careful attention to correct temperatures and cooking times. Always wait for the water to come to a boil before you start to count the sterilization time. Once the correct time has elapsed, turn off the heat, and leave the jars to cool in the pressure cooker or saucepan.

Storage
Store in a cool, dry place away from light. It is sensible to label the jars with their contents and the date.

Use by ...

How long will it keep?
It all depends on the preserving method.

Plain

Vegetables that have been bottled in water or small preserves may keep for a whole year, but if you notice mold forming on the top, don't hesitate to throw it away. Either the seal wasn't airtight or the sterilization wasn't long enough.

In salt or vinegar

Preserves using salt or vinegar, such as capers, pickles, and chutneys, are normally eaten within a month or two, but can keep for a very long time—even more than a year. However, some vegetables, such as pickled beets, and certain fish, such as salted anchovies, keep for only about 3 months. It is important, therefore, to label your preserves with dates.

In oil

Preserves using oil, like those in salt or vinegar, are normally eaten within a month or two of making. On the other hand, they can be stored for 10–12 months.

With added sugar

Preserves that use sugar, like jams and jellies, will keep very well for a long time. Syrups, such as lemon or mint, however, have to be eaten more or less right away, as they will not keep for more than a month.

In alcohol

Preserves bottled in alcohol are the ones that keep longest. In fact, the longer the fruits macerate in the alcohol, the more tender they will be. You will need to wait at least 2 months after bottling before you open the jar.

Drying

Herbs, vegetables such as mushrooms, and fruits that have been dried will keep for 6–8 months. Make sure that the fruits have thoroughly dried out and that none of them has rotted or contaminated the others. Finally, be sure to keep them in a perfectly dry place.

Making mango chutney

• To prepare a mango, cut it in half near the pit and slice into the flesh of the first half making a criss-cross pattern to produce cubes, press the skin underneath to separate the cubes, then cut the flesh from the skin. Repeat with the other half of the mango.
• Place the cubes in a dish, add brown sugar, vinegar, and spices and leave to macerate.
• Cook the mango with the sugar and spices over a very low heat.
The mixture will gradually thicken as you stir.
• Ladle the chutney into a sterilized preserving jar and seal with an airtight lid, not forgetting to use a new rubber seal.
• Turn the jar upside down to produce a vacuum.
• Store the chutney for at least 15 days before eating. It will keep for a long time if stored unopened in a dark, dry place.
Serve as an accompaniment to rice, fish, and white meat.
(See also detailed recipe page 62.)

How it works

This is basically a book for lovers of good food. The recipes that follow are easy to make, but it won't do any harm just to recall why particular techniques of preservation are considered suitable for some foods and not others. These techniques can be categorized as follows: coating, dehydration, the use of preservatives and sterilization.

Coating

Coating with fats, such as oil or duck fat, protects foods from the air. They are therefore prevented from oxidizing too quickly and becoming moldy. The fat coating also retains the moisture in the food. Because the food does not dry out, it looks better longer.

Dehydration

The drying process removes all the moisture from fruits and vegetables to stop them from going bad. They can be dried naturally in the sun, placed in an oven with the door left ajar, or dried over a stove.

Using preservatives

Preserving in salt, alcohol, vinegar, or sugar halts the development of microbes.
Make sure that you use the right type of product: sea salt is better than mineral salt; vinegar should be strong (7%); spirits are best if between 48% and 52%; use refined sugar, such as preserving, granulated or fruit sugar. Avoid brown sugar, confectioners' sugar or raw sugar, even if these are what you normally prefer.

Sterilization

Plain preserves always need to be sterilized. Use boiling water or a pressure cooker. The heat drives the air from the jars, thereby preventing molds from developing.
Sterilization times vary according to whether you use a saucepan or pressure cooker.
The times given in the recipes should be calculated from the moment the water boils.
If you use a pressure cooker, the times indicated should be reduced by one-third.

Bottling…

• Cherries in alcohol

Place the cherries in a sterilized preserving jar and cover them with sugar and eau de vie (colorless brandy), grappa or vodka, to within ¾–1½ inches of the top. Seal and store in a dark, dry place. (See also recipe page 142.)

• Dried tomatoes in oil

Place the dried tomatoes in a sterilized preserving jar. Pour in olive oil until the tomatoes are completely covered. Seal and store the jar in a dark, dry place. Once the jar has been opened, keep the tomatoes covered with oil to prevent them from drying out. (See also recipe page 16.)

• Anchovies in salt

Place anchovy fillets in a sterilized preserving jar, making alternate layers of fish and salt until the jar is completely filled. Seal and store in a dark, dry place. (See also recipe page 18.)

• Moroccan preserved lemons

Wash the lemons, slash the rind with a sharp knife and fill the slashes with coarse sea salt. Pack into a sterilized preserving jar, add 1 tablespoon coarse sea salt and seal. Place the jar in a dark, dry place. (See also recipe page 74.)

• Sun-dried mushrooms

Using a needle and thread, pierce each mushroom near the base of the stalk and make a chain of them, knotting the thread after each mushroom so that they stay separate and do not fall on one another. Wrap the mushroom-chain in cheesecloth and dry in the sun. When dry—wait at least 15 days—pack the mushrooms in a jar.

preserving in
olive oil

Fennel Oil

10 black peppercorns
5 juniper berries
12 fennel sprigs
3 cups olive oil

Drop the peppercorns and juniper berries into a glass bottle. Carefully add the fennel sprigs, then fill with olive oil. Seal the bottle with a cork and leave to infuse for at least 2 weeks.

TIP: This oil is delicious with potato salad and pickled herrings, or can also be used in a marinade for salmon.

Garlic and Basil Oil

2 basil sprigs
3 garlic cloves
8 black peppercorns
4 coriander seeds
3 cups olive oil

Carefully remove the leaves from the basil sprigs and leave them to dry in the sun or in your kitchen for about 24 hours. Put them into a glass bottle and add the garlic. Drop in the peppercorns and coriander seeds, then fill the bottle with olive oil. Seal with a cork and leave to infuse for at least 2 weeks.

TIP: You can use this oil in a dressing for tomato salad or crudités, or for flavoring pan-fried steak or brushing on to meat before grilling.

Red Chili Oil

about 10 small dried red chilies
4–5 thyme sprigs
3 oregano sprigs
10 black peppercorns
3 cups olive oil

Put the chilies into a glass bottle. Carefully add the thyme and oregano sprigs. Drop in the black peppercorns, then fill the bottle with olive oil. Seal with a cork and leave to infuse for at least 2 weeks.

TIP: This spicy chili-flavored oil is a delicious accompaniment to pizza, plain grilled fish, or potato salad.

Oregano Oil

2–3 fresh oregano sprigs
or 2 tablespoons dried oregano
3 cups olive oil

Wash the oregano and gently pat it dry in a kitchen towel or with paper towels. Drop the oregano sprigs into a bottle, then fill with olive oil. Seal with a cork, put the bottle in a dry, dark place, and leave for about 10 days before using.

TIP: This oil is excellent with pasta or pizza, or to flavor grilled white meat.

Basil Oil

2–3 fresh basil sprigs
3 cups olive oil

Wash the basil, then pat it dry in a kitchen towel or with paper towels. Drop the basil sprigs into a bottle, and fill with olive oil. Seal with a cork, put the bottle in a dry, dark place and leave for about 10 days before using.

TIP: This oil is a delicious seasoning for raw tomatoes and tomato sauces.

Garlic Oil

4 garlic cloves, crushed
3 cups olive oil

Drop the garlic into the bottle and fill with olive oil. Seal with a cork, put the bottle in a dry, dark place, and leave for about 10 days before using.

TIP: This oil is equally good for seasoning pasta, slices of grilled meat, or vegetable soup.

Goat Cheese in Olive Oil

Preparation time: 5 minutes
No cooking required

10 small, fresh goat cheeses
2 thyme sprigs
1 small bay leaf
12 black peppercorns
3 cups olive oil

Place the goat cheeses in a preserving jar.
Add the thyme, bay leaf, and peppercorns.
Cover with olive oil. Seal the jar with an
airtight lid and leave it in a cool place, but
not the refrigerator, as the cold will make
the oil congeal. Leave for about 10 days
before eating the cheeses.

TIP: Moisten some slices of crusty bread with
the aromatic oil and serve them along with
the goat cheeses.

Miniature Goat Cheese with Rosemary

Preparation time: 5 minutes
No cooking required

2–3 fresh rosemary sprigs
about 10 small goat cheeses
3 cups olive oil

Wash the rosemary, then pat it dry in a kitchen
towel or with paper towels. Place a few of the
goat cheeses at the bottom of a preserving jar,
then cover with rosemary sprigs. Add another
layer of cheeses and cover with rosemary.
Continue in the same way until all the cheeses
are in the jar. Pour in the olive oil, making sure
that it covers the cheeses. Seal the jar with an
airtight lid, then leave in a dark, dry place for
about 10 days before opening.

Goat Cheese with Garlic and Savory

Preparation time: 5 minutes
No cooking required

3 savory sprigs
about 10 small goat cheeses
2 garlic cloves
3 cups olive oil

Wash the savory, then pat it dry in a kitchen towel
or with paper towels. Place some of the goat
cheeses at the bottom of a preserving jar and
cover with savory sprigs. Add a garlic clove, then
place another layer of cheeses on top, and
sprinkle with savory. Continue making layers in
the same way until all the cheeses are in the jar.
Pour in the olive oil, ensuring that it covers the
cheeses. Seal the jar with an airtight lid and leave
in a dark place for about 10 days before opening.

Goat Cheese in Olive Oil

Tuna-stuffed Red Bell Peppers in Oil

Preparation time: 15 minutes
Cooking time: 2 minutes

1½ cups small red bell peppers
1 large can of tuna in oil
1 teaspoon black peppercorns
2 bay leaves
3 cups olive oil

Slit the peppers along one side and deseed.
Bring a large saucepan of water to a boil,
and drop in the peppers. Simmer for 2 minutes,
then drain. Flake the tuna with a fork and use
it to stuff the peppers. Place the peppers in a
preserving jar with the peppercorns and bay
leaves. Cover with olive oil and seal the jar
with an airtight lid. Store in a dark place.

Dried Tomatoes in Oil

Preparation time: 15 minutes
Cooking time: 1½ hours

3 cups small, very ripe tomatoes, halved and
deseeded
1 bay leaf
1 tablespoon white wine vinegar
3 cups olive oil

Place the tomatoes in a preheated oven, 250°F,
for about 1½ hours, then remove from the oven
and leave to cool.
Put the tomatoes in a preserving jar with the bay
leaf. Pour in the vinegar and cover with olive oil.
Seal the jar with an airtight lid.
Leave in a dark place, checking from time to
time to ensure that the tomatoes are still
covered in oil. Once the jar is opened, store
in a cool place.

TIP: This recipe is even better if you can sun-dry
your tomatoes, as people do in many
Mediterranean countries such as Italy, Spain, and
Tunisia. To do this, place the quartered tomatoes
on a tray and expose them directly to the sun,
at the same time taking care to ensure that they
are protected from dust. Leave them for several
days, turning them over regularly, and bringing
them inside every night to avoid damp.

Tuna-stuffed Red Bell Peppers in Oil

Anchovy Double

In Salt

Preparation time: 45 minutes + 8 days standing
No cooking required

2 lbs anchovies
4½ cups cooking salt
peppercorns
bay leaves
cloves

Rinse the anchovies in cold water, then drain well. Using a small, sharp knife, cut off the heads and filet the fish.
Place the anchovies in a large, shallow dish and cover with half the cooking salt. Stir well to make sure that they are thoroughly coated in salt. Leave overnight.
Sterilize a preserving jar by placing it in a large pan of boiling water for 5 minutes, then place it upside down on a clean kitchen towel to drain. Pour a layer of cooking salt into the bottom of the dry jar and arrange some anchovies, belly side down, on top. Add 6 peppercorns, ½ bay leaf and 2 cloves. Spoon in another layer of salt, then add another layer of anchovies with peppercorns, ½ bay leaf, and cloves on top. Continue making layers in this way until the jar is full.
Close the lid of the jar and place a weight on top. Leave for 1 week in a cool, dark place. Open the jar and remove the oil that has formed on the surface. Pour in a little cooking salt in its place. Seal the jar with an airtight lid and leave it in a cool, dark place.
Store for about 3 weeks before opening and eating the salted anchovies.

TIP: You can use the anchovies as you need them, taking care to rinse them under cold running water, remove their backbones, and leave them to soak for at least 1 hour in a bowl of cold water.

In Oil

After you have left the anchovies in salt for 1 week, remove the anchovy filets, one at a time, and wipe each of them with paper towels. Sterilize a preserving jar for 5 minutes in a large saucepan of boiling water, then place it upside down on a clean kitchen towel to drain.
Put the anchovy filets in the dry jar, and cover them with olive oil. Close and sterilize the jar for 1½ hours, then leave it to cool. Sterilize for an additional 30 minutes the following day.

TIP: You can put these anchovies in a salade niçoise or pan-bagnat—both specialties from the south of France. You can also use them to make anchovy butter, or purée them and serve them in an anchoïade with fresh vegetables.

Anchovies in Oil

Cook's tips

Marinated Feta

Cut some feta cheese into small cubes. Sterilize a preserving jar, then leave it upside down on a clean kitchen towel to drain. Put the feta in the dry jar, cover with an aromatic olive oil, and seal. You can use this feta to liven up your salads.

Farfalle Salad

To vary pasta salads, add some drained diced Dried Tomatoes in Oil (see page 16), diced celery, and some capers, then season with a good olive oil vinaigrette.

Oil for Pizza

To spice up your pizza parties, offer your guests some Red Chili Oil (see page 12). Be careful though—as time goes by it gets hotter and hotter, so just a few drops will be enough.

Mini-pizzas

Use a cookie cutter to stamp out 12 circles of pizza dough. Cover the dough circles with a garlic and onion tomato sauce that you have prepared earlier. Lay a slice of mozzarella on each piece, and sprinkle with chopped oregano. Add a strip of green, red, or yellow bell pepper and an olive. Finally, brush the mini-pizzas with olive oil. Cook for about 12 minutes in a preheated oven, 400°F.

Barbecuing

In the barbecue season, dip a pastry brush in some Garlic and Basil Oil (see page 12), and lightly brush some pork chops on both sides. Barbecue them for about 12 minutes, turning them over halfway through the cooking time. Serve immediately with a green salad.

Tomatoes with Mozzarella

Slice some tomatoes, then cover with slices of mozzarella, and sprinkle with Basil Oil (see page 12). Season with salt and pepper, and top with more tomato slices. Serve immediately. You can also add some black olives and a few fresh basil leaves.

Potato Salad

Peel some boiled potatoes while they are still warm. Cut them into round slices. Add 6 small green onions cut into quarters, then toss lightly with a vinaigrette made with Oregano Oil (see page 12). You can also give extra flavor to your salad by adding a small amount of chopped garlic.

Carpaccio of Beef

Put a piece of filet mignon in the freezer for 10–15 minutes to firm it, then cut it into wafer-thin slices. Lightly brush a large plate with Basil Oil (see page 12). Arrange the beef slices on the plate, brush with more oil, then season to taste with salt and pepper.

TIP: You can also sprinkle on a little coarsely grated Parmesan cheese.

Spicy Shrimp

Place some cooked peeled shrimp in a deep dish. In a bowl, mix together some olive oil and Red Chili Oil (see page 12) to taste. Pour the mixture over the shrimp and leave to marinate for at least 2 hours.

TIP: You can serve the shrimp just as they are with pre-dinner drinks, or use them to add interest to a green salad or fried rice.

Marinated Chicken Drumsticks

Place some chicken drumsticks in a deep dish. In a pitcher, mix together some Garlic Oil (see page 12) and Red Chili Oil (see page 12), using about twice as much of the former as the latter. Pour the mixture over the drumsticks to cover. Add some chopped cilantro leaves. Leave to marinate for at least 2 hours, then cook the drumsticks in the oven or on the barbecue.

Diced Cod with Fennel Oil

Cut a filet of cod into large cubes, place in a deep dish, and cover with Fennel Oil (see page 12). Leave to marinate for at least 2 hours. Cook a chopped onion in oil until lightly browned, add the cubes of marinated fish, and cook over a medium heat until tender. Season to taste with salt and pepper.

TIP: Just before serving, sprinkle with lemon juice and a little chopped fresh fennel.

Carpaccio of Beef

Fennel Salmon with Mustard Sauce

Preparation time: 10 minutes
+ 2 hours marinating
No cooking required
4 servings

2 cups sliced smoked salmon
Fennel Oil (see page 12)
1 tablespoon crushed white peppercorns
For the sauce
1 teaspoon fruit sugar
1 teaspoon chopped fennel
1 tablespoon mild mustard
1 teaspoon white wine vinegar
4 tablespoons sunflower oil

Arrange the salmon slices in a large, deep dish. Pour over fennel oil to cover and sprinkle with the crushed white peppercorns. Cover with plastic wrap and refrigerate for at least 2 hours. Just before serving, prepare the sauce. Mix together the sugar, chopped fennel, and mustard in a bowl, add the vinegar, then gradually pour in the sunflower oil, stirring constantly. Serve the fish with the sauce.

Fennel Salmon with Mustard Sauce

Grilled Garlic Chicken Breasts

Preparation time: 10 minutes
Cooking time: 6 minutes
4 servings

2 skinless boneless chicken breasts, cut into
thin strips
1 tablespoon Garlic Oil (see page 12)
a few basil leaves
1 cup lettuce leaves
3 small white onions, thinly sliced
3 tablespoons olive oil
1½ teaspoons Honey Vinegar (see page 36)
salt and pepper

Brush the chicken strips with a little garlic oil
and season with salt and pepper.
Broil or grill, turning frequently, for about
6 minutes, until golden on all sides.
Meanwhile, place the basil leaves and lettuce
in a large salad bowl and add the onions.
Whisk together the olive oil and vinegar in a
pitcher. Pour the dressing over the salad, then
season lightly with salt and pepper. Toss well to
mix. Arrange the grilled chicken strips on the
salad and serve immediately.

Grilled Garlic Chicken Breasts

Broiled Goat Cheese on Toast

Preparation time: 5 minutes
Cooking time: 4–5 minutes
4 servings

4 slices of crusty bread
or ½ baguette
2 cabécou or other individual goat
cheeses marinated in oil, drained, and
halved horizontally
pepper

Lightly toast the bread on one side under
the broiler. Remove from the heat and arrange
the cheese on top. Return to the oven
and broil until the cheese has melted.
Season lightly with pepper and serve with
a mixed green or arugula salad.

Broiled Goat Cheese on Toast

Dried Tomato and Olive Oil Paste

Preparation time: 15 minutes
No cooking required

1 cup dried tomatoes
1 cup water
1 bay leaf
olive oil

Place the dried tomatoes in a small pan, add the measured water, and heat gently for about 10 minutes. Transfer to a blender or food processor and process to a thick paste.
If necessary add a little extra water.
Pour the tomato paste into a preserving jar and add the bay leaf. Cover with a little olive oil. Seal the jar with an airtight lid and store in a dark cupboard. Once the jar has been opened, keep the tomato and olive oil paste in a cool place.

Pizzas with Dried Tomato Paste and Anchovies

Preparation time: 20 minutes
+ 1 hour rising time for the dough
Cooking time: 12 minutes
4 servings

Garlic Oil (see page 12)
Dried Tomato and Olive Oil Paste (see left)
20 canned anchovy filets, drained
1 teaspoon oregano
olive oil, for brushing

For the dough
1 package baker's yeast
½ cup lukewarm water
2 cups all-purpose flour
1 tablespoon olive oil
salt

First, make the dough. Mix the yeast with 2 tablespoons of the water in a small bowl. Put the flour and a pinch of salt into a food processor, add the yeast mixture, and process to mix. With the motor running, gradually add the remaining water and the olive oil. As soon as the mixture comes together, turn out the dough and knead until smooth and elastic. Place the dough on a cookie sheet, cover with a kitchen towel, and leave to rise in a warm, draft-free place for about 1 hour, or until doubled in volume.
Brush a cookie sheet with oil, then sprinkle lightly with flour.
Divide the dough into 4 equal pieces and place on the cookie sheet. Gently flatten with your hand to form 4 balls of equal size. Set the balls aside for about 10 minutes.
Brush the dough balls with garlic oil, then spread the tomato paste over them.
Divide the anchovy filets among the pizzas, sprinkle with oregano, and brush with olive oil. Bake in a preheated oven, 400°F, for about 12 minutes. Serve immediately.

Pizzas with Dried Tomato Paste and Anchovies

preserving
in vinegar

Myrtle and Blackberry Vinegar

1 handful of blackberries, preferably wild
1 small myrtle sprig
4 cups wine vinegar

Gently insert the blackberries and sprig of myrtle into a bottle, pour in wine vinegar, and seal the bottle well.
Store in a dark, dry place.
Leave for about 3 weeks before using.

TIP: Excellent for deglazing the roasting pan after cooking game. It is worth trying to obtain myrtle for this recipe, as it is a lovely, fragrant, spicy herb, but it is not widely available. You could substitute rosemary or lavender instead.

Rosemary Vinegar

1 large rosemary sprig
4 cups wine vinegar

Put the rosemary sprig into the bottle,
pour in the vinegar, and seal the bottle well.
Store in a dark, dry place.
Leave for at least 3 weeks before using.

TIP: Excellent with grilled or pan-fried meat or with steamed fish.

Basil Vinegar

1 large basil sprig
4 cups wine vinegar

Place the basil in a bottle, pour in the vinegar, and seal well.
Store in a dark, dry place.
Leave for at least 3 weeks before using.

TIP: This vinegar makes an excellent salad dressing with olive oil.

Tarragon Vinegar

5 tarragon sprigs
4 cups wine vinegar

Dry the sprigs of tarragon in a dark, dry place for 1 week.
Insert the dried tarragon into a bottle, pour in the vinegar, and seal the bottle well.
Store in a dark, dry place.
Leave for at least 3 weeks before using.

TIP: This vinegar goes well in robust salads, with chicken dishes, or as a seasoning for fried eggs.

Rosemary Vinegar; Myrtle and Blackberry Vinegar

Honey Vinegar

4 tablespoons clear honey
4 cups cider vinegar

Pour the honey and vinegar into a bottle and seal well.
Store the bottle in a dark, dry place.
Leave for about 3 weeks before using.

TIP: This vinegar is delicious in salad dressings, good for spicing up apple sauce, and can also be used to deglaze roasting pans for making gravy—especially with duck.

Fruit Vinegar

1 handful of slightly underripe berries, such as strawberries or raspberries
5 small bay leaves
4 cups wine vinegar

Put the berries and bay leaves in a bottle, pour in the vinegar, and seal the bottle well.
Store in a dark, dry place.
Leave about 3 weeks before using.

TIP: Excellent in a vinaigrette or to season a fresh green salad. The berries will go on ripening in the bottle and will end up a very attractive red.

Honey Vinegar

Pickled Onions

Pickled Cherries

Pickled Onions

Preparation time: 20 minutes + cooling
Cooking time: 5 minutes

2 cups pickling onions
1 clove
1 bay leaf
5 black peppercorns
2 cups white wine vinegar

Bring a saucepan of water to a boil. Add the
onions and boil for 2 minutes. Drain well and
place them in a preserving jar with the clove,
bay leaf, and peppercorns.
Pour the vinegar into a thick saucepan. Bring
to a boil and boil for 3 minutes, then remove
from the heat and leave to cool.
Pour the vinegar into the jar to cover the onions
and seal the jar with an airtight lid.
Store in a dark, dry place for about 2 months
before consuming.

Pickled Cherries

Preparation time: 10 minutes + cooling
Cooking time: 5 minutes

2 cups cherries
2 cups cider vinegar
½ cup sugar
2 cloves
¼ cinnamon stick
¼ teaspoon ground nutmeg

Place the cherries in a preserving jar.
Pour the vinegar into a thick saucepan
and add the sugar, cloves, cinnamon, and
nutmeg. Bring to a boil and boil for 3 minutes,
then remove from the heat and leave to cool.
Pour the vinegar mixture into the jar to cover
the cherries and seal the jar with an airtight lid.
Store in a dark, dry, place for about 2 months
before consuming the cherries.

Pickled Gherkins with Tarragon

Preparation time: 25 minutes
+ overnight standing
No cooking required

4 cups small gherkins, trimmed
2 cups coarse sea salt
4 shallots
10 fresh or dried tarragon sprigs
15 black peppercorns
15 coriander seeds
3 cups distilled malt vinegar

Rub the gherkins vigorously with a towel to
remove any down.
Place them in a large bowl and cover with
the salt, mixing well to ensure that they are
thoroughly coated. Leave overnight for the
juices to drain.
Next day, drain the gherkins and pat dry with
a kitchen towel or paper towels.
Put the gherkins into preserving jars. Divide the
shallots, tarragon, peppercorns, and coriander
seeds among the jars. Pour in the vinegar and
seal the jars with airtight lids.
Store in a dark, dry place for 6–8 weeks before
eating the pickles.

TIP: These pickles are delicious with pâté or
cold meat. They can also be added, cut into
pieces, to a potato salad garnished with a
shallot vinaigrette. Some people like to heat the
vinegar before pouring it over the gherkins, but
the use of cold vinegar appears to produce a
tastier result: the pickles are then incomparably
crunchy.

Pickled Gherkins with Tarragon

Spiced Pickled Red Cabbage

**Preparation time: 20 minutes
+ overnight standing
Cooking time: 3 minutes**

12 cups red cabbage, cored and shredded
4 cups red wine vinegar
10 black peppercorns
4 bay leaves
6 cloves
salt

Place the cabbage in a large terrine and cover
with salt. Mix well and leave overnight.
Next day, drain the cabbage and pat dry with
paper towels to remove the salt. Pour the vinegar
and spices into a thick saucepan. Bring to a boil
and boil for 3 minutes; then remove
the saucepan from the heat. Pack the cabbage
strips into preserving jars and pour in the spiced
vinegar to cover. Seal the jars with airtight lids.
Store in a dark, dry place for at least 2 weeks
before eating.
This makes a great garnish with a meat pie.

Pickled Beets

**Preparation time: 20 minutes + cooling
Cooking time: about 2½ hours**

1 lb beets
2 cups wine vinegar
1 clove
1 bay leaf
5 black peppercorns
salt

Sterilize a preserving jar in a large saucepan of
boiling water for 5 minutes, then put it upside
down to drain on a clean kitchen towel.
Put the beets in a saucepan and add water to
cover. Add a pinch of salt and bring to a boil.
Lower the heat and simmer for 2 hours, until
tender. Check by inserting the point of a sharp
knife in the thickest part; it should slide in easily.
Remove the beets from the saucepan and
leave to cool. Peel and slice.
Place the slices in the dry jar with the clove, bay
leaf, and peppercorns. Pour the wine vinegar into
a heavy-based saucepan. Bring to a boil and boil
for 3 minutes, then remove from the heat.
Pour the vinegar into the jar to cover the beets
and seal the jar with an airtight lid.
Store in a dark, dry place for 2 weeks before
consuming.

Pickled Beets

Pickled Pearl Onions

Preparation time: 20 minutes
+ 2 hours standing
Cooking time: 15 minutes

2 cups pearl onions
4 tablespoons coarse sea salt
2 cups cider vinegar
1 teaspoon mustard seeds
1 teaspoon coriander seeds
3 cloves
½ cinnamon stick
5 black peppercorns

Bring a large saucepan of water to a boil, add the onions and cook for 2 minutes. Drain well, place in a dish, and cover them with the sea salt. Set aside for about 2 hours.

Pour the cider vinegar into a saucepan and add the mustard seeds, coriander seeds, cloves, cinnamon, and the peppercorns. Bring to a boil and boil for about 3 minutes. Remove the pan from the heat and leave to cool.

Rinse the onions to remove the salt, then place them in a thick saucepan. Pour in the spiced vinegar and bring to a boil. Simmer for about 6 minutes, then remove the pan from the heat. Pack the onions in a preserving jar, pour in spiced vinegar to cover, and seal with an airtight lid. Store in a dark, dry place for at least 2 weeks before consuming.

Miniature Pickled Vegetables

Preparation time: 20 minutes
Cooking time: 10 minutes

1¼ cup French beans, cut into 1 inch lengths
1¼ cup pearl onions
1¼ cup cauliflower florets
2 cups malt vinegar
1 teaspoon dry mustard
1 teaspoon grated fresh root ginger

Sterilize a jar in a saucepan of boiling water for 5 minutes, then put it upside down to drain on a clean kitchen towel.

Bring a large pan of salted water to a boil, add the French beans, onions, and cauliflower and cook for 2 minutes. Drain well and place the vegetables in a preserving jar.

Pour the malt vinegar into a saucepan and add the mustard and ginger. Bring to a boil, then lower the heat and simmer for about 3 minutes. Remove the pan from the heat and strain the vinegar into a pitcher. Pour the vinegar into the jar to cover the miniature vegetables, then seal the jar with an airtight lid.

Store in a dark dry place for at least 2 weeks before using.

TIP: You can pickle other vegetables in the same way. Try baby corn cobs, slices of carrot, small gherkins, and chunks of red bell pepper.

Miniature Pickled Vegetables

Pickled Mushrooms

**Preparation time: 20 minutes + cooling
Cooking time: 20 minutes**

10 cups mushrooms
1 cup white wine vinegar
1 cup white wine
1 cup water
1 thyme sprig
½ teaspoon mustard seeds
3 black peppercorns
2 tablespoons fruit sugar
1¼ teaspoons salt

Cut any large mushrooms into quarters.
Pour the vinegar, wine, and water into a thick saucepan. Add the thyme, mustard seeds, peppercorns, sugar, and salt.
Bring to a boil and add the mushrooms. Lower the heat and simmer for about 8 minutes.
Remove the mushrooms with a slotted spoon, and continue to simmer the vinegar mixture for an additional 5 minutes, until reduced. Remove from the heat and leave to cool.
Sterilize a preserving jar in a large saucepan of boiling water for 5 minutes, then put it upside down to drain on a clean kitchen towel. Fill the jar with the mushrooms and pour in the cooled vinegar mixture. Seal the jar with an airtight lid. Store in a dark, dry place.

TIP: These mushrooms are an excellent garnish for dry-cured ham.

Chanterelle Mushrooms in Vinegar

**Preparation time: 15 minutes
Cooking time: 1 hour**

10 cups small chanterelle mushrooms
1 shallot
1 thyme sprig
5 peppercorns
1¼ teaspoons salt
1 cup white wine vinegar
1 cup water

Cut any large mushrooms in half, then place all the mushrooms in a preserving jar. Add the shallot, thyme, peppercorns, and salt.
Pour the vinegar and water into a thick saucepan. Bring to a boil, then lower the heat, and simmer for 2–3 minutes. Pour the mixture into the jar and seal with an airtight lid.
Place the jar in a large saucepan, add enough water to cover, and bring to a boil. Boil for 1 hour. Remove the jar from the pan and leave to cool completely.
Store the jar in a dark, dry place.

TIP: These mushrooms make an excellent garnish for pork dishes.

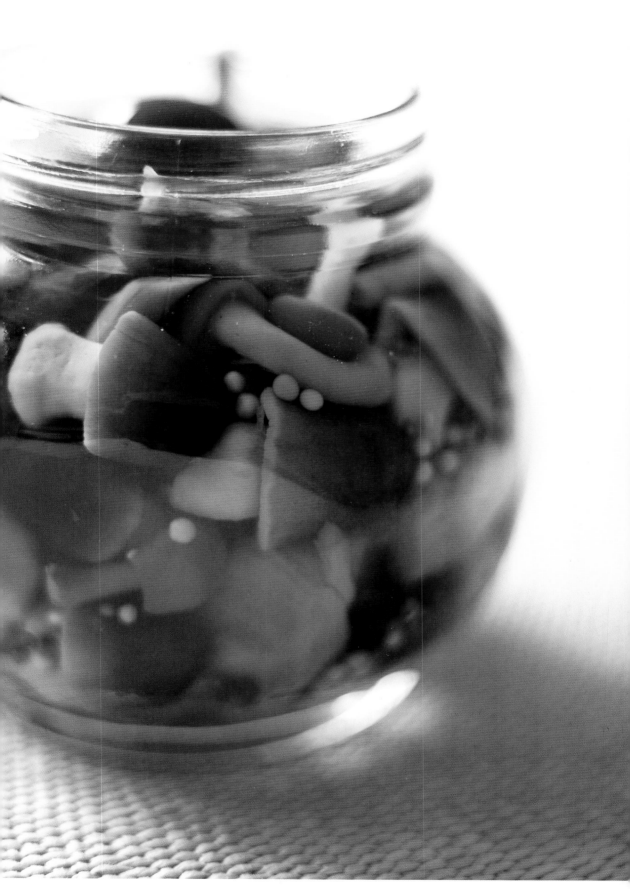

Pickled Mushrooms

Cook's tips

Home-pickled Gherkins

For lunch on the run, you can't beat the traditional crusty sandwich, with fresh French bread, good-quality salami or salt beef, unsalted butter, and a handful of Pickled Gherkins with Tarragon (see page 40). They are also incomparable on a platter of cold meats. Try them, too, with venison or other strongly flavored pâté.

Fruit Vinegar

For a pleasant change, substitute the delicate taste of Fruit Vinegar (see page 36) for wine vinegar when dressing a green salad. You will better appreciate its fragrance if you prepare the vinaigrette with a neutral tasting oil, such as sunflower oil, for instance.

Pickled Cherries

Pickled Cherries (see page 40) have
a unique sharp crunchiness. They lend
piquancy to cold meats and are a
marvelous accompaniment to a good
terrine or coarse pâté.

Pickled Mushrooms

You could surprise guests by serving
Pickled Mushrooms (see page 46) on
cocktail sticks with predinner drinks.
You could then go on to serve them
as a first course garnish to spice up
game pâté, for example.

Pickled Onions

You have some leftover roast beef?
Now's the time to get out your
Pickled Pearl Onions (see page 44).

Fried Egg with Fruit Vinegar

Preparation time: 5 minutes
Cooking time: 2–3 minutes
1 Serving

pat of butter
½ teaspoon sunflower oil
1 or 2 eggs
Fruit Vinegar (see page 36)
salt and pepper

Melt the butter with the oil in a small, nonstick frying pan.
Crack the egg or eggs into it and cook over a low heat for a few minutes, until the white is cooked and set but the yollk is still runny. Season lightly with salt and pepper and transfer to a plate. Add a dash of fruit vinegar and serve.

TIP: This is even more delicious served with crusty country bread or fresh French bread.

Fried Egg with Fruit Vinegar

Straight from the cupboard

Tarragon Vinaigrette with Shallots

1 teaspoon Dijon mustard
1 tablespoon Tarragon Vinegar (see page 34)
3 tablespoons sunflower oil
1 shallot, chopped
salt and pepper

Place the mustard and vinegar in a bowl, season with salt, and stir briskly with a fork or small whisk. Gradually add the oil, whisking constantly until thoroughly combined. Add the chopped shallot and season with pepper. Use immediately to dress a potato salad, for example.

Garlic and Rosemary Vinaigrette

1 tablespoon Rosemary Vinegar (see page 34)
3 tablespoons Garlic Oil (see page 12)
salt and pepper

Pour the vinegar into a bowl, season with salt and beat well. Gradually add the oil, whisking constantly until thoroughly combined. Season with pepper and use immediately to dress a green salad, for example.

Curry-flavored Vinaigrette

2 teaspoons curry powder
1 tablespoon white wine vinegar
3 tablespoons Garlic Oil (see page 12)
salt and pepper

Put the curry powder and vinegar in a bowl, season with salt, and stir well with a fork or small whisk. Gradually add the oil, stirring constantly until thoroughly combined. Season with pepper, and use immediately to dress a beet or potato salad, or steamed leeks.

52   Preserving in vinegar

Curry-flavored Vinaigrette

Duck Fillets with Honey Vinegar

Preparation time: 5 minutes
Cooking time: 15 minutes
4 Servings

2 duck breast fillets
1 tablespoon Honey Vinegar (see page 36)
salt and pepper

Lightly score the skin of the duck breasts with a small, sharp knife.
Season the flesh side of the duck with salt and pepper. Heat a heavy frying pan. Add the duck breasts, skin side down and cook for about 10 minutes.
Drain off the fat from the pan and turn the duck breasts over. Cook for an additional 3–4 minutes, then remove the duck breasts from the pan, and keep warm.
Drain off the fat from the pan and pour in the honey vinegar. Heat gently, scraping the pan with a wooden spoon to release the meat juices into the vinegar.
Pour the honey vinegar-flavored juices over the duck and serve immediately.

TIP: Depending on season and price, you can vary the choice of vegetables served with this dish.

Pickled Vegetable Mini-kebabs

Preparation time: 20 minutes
+ overnight standing
Cooking time: 10 minutes

1½ cups small gherkins
1½ cups red bell peppers, cut in half and deseeded
1½ cups carrots, cut into quarters
1½ cups pearl onions
4 cups distilled malt vinegar
10 black peppercorns
salt

Put the gherkins in a large dish and cover with a fine layer of salt. Put the bell pepper halves in another dish and cover with a fine layer of salt. The following day, wipe the peppers with paper towels to remove the excess salt, then cut them into small squares. Wipe the gherkins.
Bring a large saucepan of water to a boil, add the carrots, and cook for 3–4 minutes. Drain well. Cook the pearl onions in a pan of boiling water for 1 minute, then drain well.
Thread the vegetables onto small wooden skewers, alternating carrots, onions, pepper squares, and gherkins.
Place the mini-kebabs together vertically in large preserving jars. Pour in the vinegar and add the peppercorns. Seal the jars with airtight lids.
Store in a dark place for about 3 weeks before serving the mini-kebabs, which will be delicious either as hors d'oeuvres with predinner drinks or as an accompaniment to cold meat or pâté.

TIP: If you have any pickled mushrooms, such as small chanterelles, add these to your kebabs. You can add pitted olives too.

Pickled Vegetable Mini-kebabs

sweet-and-sour preserves

Onion Marmalade

Preparation time: 10 minutes
Cooking time: 45 minutes

2½ cups onions, thinly sliced
½ cup wine vinegar
1 cup red wine
½ cup fruit sugar
1 cup grenadine
salt and pepper

Place the onions in a large, nonstick frying pan, cover and cook over a very low heat for about 10 minutes.
Pour in the vinegar and red wine, increase the heat to high, and cook, uncovered, for 5 minutes, until reduced.
Lower the heat and add the sugar and grenadine. Season with salt and pepper.
Stir well and simmer very gently for 30 minutes. The mixture will gradually thicken. Remove from the heat and leave to cool slightly.
Pour into jars and seal while still warm.

TIP: Serve the onion marmalade with cold meat or duck pâté.

Sweet-and-Sour Gherkins

Preparation time: 15 minutes
Cooking time: 40 minutes

¼ cup carrot, sliced
1 white onion, thinly sliced
a few fennel sprigs
5 coriander seeds
5 black peppercorns
1 lb large gherkins
½ cup white wine vinegar
2 cups water
2 tablespoons fruit sugar
1½ teaspoons fine salt

Sterilize a preserving jar in a large pan of boiling water for 5 minutes. Leave upside down to drain on a kitchen towel. Put the carrot and onion slices into the dry jar with the fennel, coriander seeds, peppercorns, and gherkins.
Pour the vinegar and water into a thick saucepan and add the sugar and salt. Bring to a boil, then immediately remove the pan from the heat. Leave the brine to cool slightly, then pour into the jar to cover the vegetables. Seal the jar, place in a large saucepan of water and bring to a boil. Boil for about 30 minutes.
Leave the jar to cool in the saucepan, then store it in a cool, dark place.

TIP: Wait for about 1 month before opening.

Onion Marmalade

Mostarda

Preparation time: 15 minutes
+ overnight standing
Cooking time: 20 minutes

1 cup fruit sugar
4 cups water
4 slightly firm pears, peeled, cored and cut
into chunks
4 apples, peeled, cored and cut into chunks
4 slightly firm plums
12 grapes
4 cups white wine
1⅓ cups honey
2 tablespoons dry mustard

Put the sugar into a thick saucepan, pour in the
water, and heat gently, stirring until the sugar
has dissolved.
Add the pears and apples, and then simmer for
about 10 minutes. Add the plums and grapes,
and simmer for an additional 5 minutes. Remove
from the heat, and leave the mixture overnight.
The following day, bring the contents of the pan
back to simmering point, then strain the fruits,
and pack them into preserving jars.
Pour the wine and honey into another thick
saucepan, add the mustard, and heat to
simmering point. Pour mixture into the jars to
cover the fruit and seal the jars with airtight lids.

TIP: This mostarda will keep for several weeks,
and may be served with boiled or roast meat.

Mostarda

Mango Chutney

**Preparation time: 15 minutes
+ about 3 hours standing
Cooking time: 2½ hours
Makes 2 jars (8 oz each)**

3 mangoes, peeled, pitted and diced
(see page 6)
1 cup soft brown sugar
1 pinch ground turmeric
1 teaspoon ground cinnamon
1 teaspoon grated fresh root ginger
½ teaspoon salt
2 garlic cloves, chopped
1 large onion, thinly sliced
2 cups malt or white wine vinegar

Put the mangoes, sugar, turmeric, cinnamon, and
ginger into a dish. Mix well and leave for about
2 hours.
Transfer the mixture to a thick saucepan, add the
salt, garlic, onion, and vinegar and bring to
simmering point, stirring constantly. Simmer,
stirring occasionally, for about 2½ hours, until the
chutney has thickened.
Sterilize 2 preserving jars in a large saucepan of
boiling water for 5 minutes, then remove and
place upside down on a clean kitchen towel to
drain. Leave the chutney to stand for about
20 minutes, then ladle it into the jars, and seal
with airtight lids. Turn the jars upside down.
When cool, store in a cool dark place.

TIP: You can use this chutney immediately, but
it will be even better if you leave it for a couple
of weeks. Once a jar has been opened it will
keep very well for 2 weeks in the refrigerator.

Apple and Raisin Chutney

**Preparation time: 10 minutes
+ 1½ hours standing
Cooking time: 2½ hours
Makes 3 jars (8 oz each)**

2 cups apples, peeled, quartered and cored
1 large onion, thinly sliced
1 cup raisins
1 cup soft brown sugar
1 teaspoon grated fresh root ginger
½ teaspoon salt
1 cup cider vinegar

Thinly slice the apple quarters crosswise and
place in a dish. Add the onion, raisins, sugar,
ginger, salt, and vinegar and leave for about
1 hour. Pour the contents of the dish into a thick
saucepan and heat to simmering point, stirring
constantly. Simmer, stirring occasionally, for about
2½ hours, until thickened.
Sterilize 3 preserving jars in a large saucepan of
boiling water for 5 minutes, then remove, and
place upside down to drain on a clean kitchen
towel.
Leave the chutney to stand for about 20 minutes,
then ladle it into the jars, and seal with airtight
lids. Turn the jars upside down. When cool, store
in a cool, dark place.

TIP: You can use the chutney immediately, but
it will be even better if you leave it for a couple
of weeks. Once a jar has been opened, keep it
in the refrigerator.

Mango Chutney

Orange and Date Chutney

Preparation time: 10 minutes
+ 20 minutes standing
Cooking time: 2½ hours
Makes 3 jars (8 oz each)

2 cups apples, peeled, quartered
and cored
1 cup dates, pitted and chopped
1 cup oranges, peeled and chopped
1 cup soft brown sugar
2 teaspoons grated fresh root ginger
½ teaspoon salt
1 cup malt or white wine vinegar

Slice the apples into a thick saucepan and add
the dates, oranges, sugar, ginger, salt, and
vinegar. Bring to simmering point, stirring
constantly. Simmer, stirring occasionally, for
about 2½ hours, until thickened.
Sterilize 3 preserving jars in a large saucepan of
boiling water for 5 minutes, then place upside
down on a clean kitchen towel to drain.
Leave the chutney to stand for about 20 minutes,
then ladle it into the jars, and seal with airtight
lids. Turn the jars upside down. When cool, store
in a cool, dark place.

TIP: You can use this chutney immediately, but
it will be even better if you leave it for a couple
of weeks. Once a jar has been opened it must
be kept in the refrigerator.

Orange and Date Chutney

Boiled Beef with Mostarda

If you are wondering how to use a good piece of boiled beef or some leftover braised steak, cut it into large cubes and serve it as a first course with some mustard-flavored fruits. The Mostarda (see page 60) will lift the flavor of the cold meat deliciously.

Onion Marmalade

Onion Marmalade (see page 58) is the perfect accompaniment to ham, salami, and other cold meats. It balances the flavors and is particularly good with game pâtés. You can also serve it with duck and farmhouse cheese.

Apple and Raisin Rice

Put 1 cup basmati rice into a saucepan with 1½ cups boiling water and season with salt and pepper. Cover and simmer for about 15 minutes, until tender. Strain the rice, if necessary, and serve warm with Apple and Raisin Chutney (see page 62). You could also add some slices of fresh mango.

Orange and Date Chutney

Put a boned and rolled loin of pork into a pan, cover with a mixture of milk and water, season and add 4 garlic cloves and 1 thyme sprig. Simmer, allowing 1¼ hours per 2lb meat. Drain and leave to cool. Slice and serve cold with Orange and Date Chutney (see page 64).

Sweet-and-Sour Mushrooms with Prosciutto

Sweet-and-sour mushrooms will make prosciutto, terrines, and pâtés a special treat. The wild mushrooms will lose something of their rustic simplicity, but will make up for it by bringing out the delicious flavors of your cold meats.

Turkey Breast with Mango Chutney

Cut the turkey breast into short strips, then grill or broil until tender, and serve with Mango Chutney (see page 62) as a dipping sauce. You can also use these ingredients to make an absolutely delicious sandwich.

Duck and Hazelnut Pâté

**Preparation time: 30 minutes
+ overnight marinating + 1–2 hours cooling
Cooking time: 2½ hours
Prepare the day before serving**

1 cup chicken livers
1 cup brandy
3¾ cups duck breast filets, cut into
large cubes
1 cup sausagemeat
2 cups belly pork
1 garlic clove, finely chopped
3 shallots, finely chopped
2 tablespoons chopped parsley
pinch of ground allspice
1 cup shelled and skinned
hazelnuts, coarsely crushed
3 eggs, lightly beaten
1 cup fatty bacon or bacon fat
2 bay leaves
1 thyme sprig
salt and ground white pepper

Place the chicken livers in a deep dish, pour in
the brandy, cover, and leave to marinate overnight
in a cool place.
The next day, drain the chicken livers. Put the
duck, sausagemeat, belly pork, and chicken livers
through a mincer or chop finely in a food
processor. Transfer to a bowl, if necessary.
Add the garlic, shallots, and chopped parsley.
Season with salt, pepper, and allspice, then add
the nuts and eggs. Mix thoroughly.
Place a layer of bacon or bacon fat in the bottom
of a 10-inch long terrine, and cover with the duck
mixture, packing it down firmly. Cover with
another layer of bacon or bacon fat. Decorate
with the bay leaves and the thyme sprig.
Put the terrine in a roasting pan and add boiling
water to come halfway up the sides.
Bake in a preheated oven, 325°F, for about
2½ hours, adding more boiling water if necessary.
Remove the terrine from the roasting pan and
leave to stand for 1–2 hours at room
temperature.
Cover the pâté with a small board, place a weight
on top and leave for about 12 hours. Store the
pâté in a cool place.

TIP: Serve with Onion Marmalade (see page 58).

preserving with salt

Green Olives

Moroccan Preserved Lemons

Green Olives

Preparation time: 45 minutes + cooling
Cooking time: 5 minutes

2 cups green olives
salt

Sterilize the jars in a large saucepan of boiling water for 5 minutes, then leave to drain upside down on a clean kitchen towel.
Put the olives in jars and pour in cold water to cover. Leaving the olives in the jars, pour the water into a measuring container. Stir salt into the water, in the proportion of 4½ tablespoons salt per 4 cups of water.
Pour the salted water into a saucepan and bring to a boil. Boil for about 5 minutes, then remove from the heat, and leave to cool.
Pour the salt water onto the olives making sure that they are completely covered in the liquid. Leave to macerate for about 4 weeks before consuming.

TIP: You can add aromatic interest to the olives by adding a peeled garlic clove or a few strands of fennel.
You can preserve black olives in the same way.

Moroccan Preserved Lemons

Preparation time: 10 minutes
No cooking required

10 unwaxed or thoroughly scrubbed lemons
fine salt
1 tablespoon coarse sea salt

Place lemons in a deep dish and pour in cold water to cover. Leave for about 6 days, changing the water daily. Make incisions into the rind, as if cutting them into quarters, but do not cut into the flesh. Place a good pinch of fine salt in each incision.
Sterilize a jar in a large saucepan of boiling water for 5 minutes, then place upside down to drain on a clean kitchen towel.
Pack the lemons in the jar. They should fit tightly together. Add the coarse sea salt. Seal the jar and leave to macerate for 1 month before consuming. The lemons will keep for several months.

TIP: Try serving the lemons finely diced with olives and roasted pistachios as a canapé, or slice them and simmer in a tagine (North African stew).

Salted Capers

Preparation time: 45 minutes
+ overnight standing
No cooking required

1½ cups capers
1 cup coarse sea salt
5 peppercorns

Place the capers in a dish and cover with salt. Mix well to ensure that the capers are thoroughly coated. Leave overnight.
The next day, sterilize a preserving jar in a large saucepan of boiling water for 5 minutes, then place upside down on a clean kitchen towel to drain. Place a fine layer of coarse sea salt in the base of the jar and add the capers. Add the peppercorns. Seal the jar with an airtight lid and store in a cool, dark place.

TIP: You can use these capers as you need them, making sure that you rinse them thoroughly under cold running water first. Uses include garnishing pizzas, spicing up a veal stew or pasta salad, or indeed as the essential flavor in caper sauce.
After opening, store the jar in the refrigerator.

Salted Capers

Olive Fougasse

Add 2 tablespoons of olive oil to
1 cup bread dough and knead in
4 tablespoons thinly sliced, pitted
black olives (see Tip page 74).
Shape into a rectangle and slash
the top 3–4 times. Bake for about
25 minutes in a preheated oven,
350°F.

Anchovy Potatoes

Cook whole, unpeeled potatoes in
a large saucepan of lightly salted,
boiling water with a little thyme and
bay leaves. Drain, peel, and halve.
Hollow out the cut sides very slightly
and garnish with Anchovies in Oil
(see page 18) and finely chopped
chives.

Smoked Fish Pâté and Caper Savory

This is a simple recipe for summer appetizers. Rinse some Salted Capers (see page 74) and pat dry with paper towels. Stamp out circles of bread with a cookie cutter and spread with ready-made smoked fish pâté. Place 2–3 capers on top.

Cold Meat with Samphire

If you have some leftover cold meat, cut it into slices that are not too thick, or dice it up and serve it with samphire, called by some "the asparagus of the sea."

Lemon Chicken Tagine

Preparation time: 15 minutes
Cooking time: 2 hours
4–6 servings

1 Moroccan Preserved Lemon (see page 74)
1 tablespoon olive oil
4–6 chicken pieces
2 onions, chopped
½ teaspoon ground cinnamon
2 tablespoons clear honey
1 cup chicken stock
salt and pepper
2 tablespoons Tomato Coulis (see page 96),
to serve

Bring a pan of salted water to a boil, add the lemon, and simmer for about 10 minutes. Drain well and slice.

Heat the oil on top of the stove in an ovenproof casserole, add the chicken pieces, and cook, turning frequently, until browned all over. Remove the chicken from the casserole and keep warm.

Add the onions to the casserole and cook, stirring occasionally, for about 5 minutes, until softened.

Return the chicken to the casserole, add the cinnamon, and season with salt and pepper.

Stir in the honey and stock.

Cover and cook in a preheated oven, 250°F, for about 1½ hours.

Add the lemon to the casserole, lower the oven temperature to 225°F and cook for an additional 20 minutes.

Taste and adjust the seasoning, if necessary, and serve immediately with the tomato coulis.

Lemon Chicken Tagine

specialty
preserves

Confit of Duck

**Preparation time: 15 minutes
+ overnight standing
Cooking time: 2¾ hours**

1 duck, cut into pieces including the fat
thyme sprigs
1 bay leaf
cooking salt
pepper

Weigh the duck, then place the pieces in a
large dish with the thyme and bay leaf. Add the
cooking salt, allowing about 1 tablespoon of salt
for every 1 lb of duck. The following day, remove
the pieces of duck and wipe carefully with a
kitchen towel or paper towels.
Spoon the duck fat from the dish into a large pan
and melt over a low heat. Add the pieces of meat
and cook for about 45 minutes.
Put the duck pieces into preserving jars, and cover
them with the melted duck fat. Seal the jars and
place in a large pan of boiling water. Boil for
about 2 hours, then remove from the pan, and
leave to cool.
Keep the confit for 2–3 months before eating.

Confit of Duck

Ratatouille

Preparation time: 30 minutes
Cooking time: 2 hours

about 5 tablespoons olive oil
5 small garlic cloves, chopped
4 cups onions, thinly sliced
3½ cups tomatoes, skinned, halved,
and deseeded
1 handful of basil leaves
3 pinches of thyme leaves
2½ cups eggplant, sliced
2 cups zucchini, sliced
2 cups bell peppers, deseeded and sliced into
fine strips
salt and pepper

Sterilize the preserving jars in a large pan of
boiling water for 10 minutes. Remove and place
upside down on a clean kitchen towel to drain.
Heat 2 tablespoons of the olive oil in a pan and
add the garlic, onions, tomatoes, basil, and
thyme.
Cook over a low heat for about 15 minutes, until
the tomatoes are thick and pulpy.
Heat 1 tablespoon of the remaining oil in another
pan. Add the eggplant slices and cook, turning
frequently, until lightly golden. Season lightly with
salt, then remove from the pan, and set aside.
Add the zucchini slices to the pan, with the
remaining oil, if necessary. Cook over a medium
heat for about 10 minutes, until lightly golden,
then season lightly with salt. Remove the zucchini
from the pan and set aside.
Add the pepper strips to the pan and cook for
about 10 minutes. Season lightly with salt.
Return all the vegetables to the pan, stir in the
tomato mixture, season generously with pepper,
and simmer for 35 minutes.
Ladle the ratatouille into the jars, leaving a
1–1½ inch headspace at the top of each jar.
Seal the jars with airtight lids. Place in a large
saucepan, pour in water to cover, and bring
to a boil. Boil for 45 minutes.
Leave the jars to cool in the water in the pan,
then store in a dark, dry place.

Ratatouille

Cassoulet

**Preparation time: 30 minutes
+ overnight standing
Cooking time: 2¾ hours**

2 cups beans (e.g. kidney or haricot), soaked in
cold water overnight and drained
½ cup lightly salted belly pork
1 bouquet garni
1 Toulouse sausage or other garlic-flavored
cooking sausage
1 tablespoon duck fat
3 pieces of Confit of Duck (see page 82)
2 cups boned shoulder of lamb, cut into large
cubes
2 onions, chopped
4 garlic cloves, crushed
6 tomatoes, skinned, seeded, and finely chopped
salt and pepper

Place the beans, belly pork, and bouquet garni in
a large saucepan and pour in water to cover.
Bring to a boil, then lower the heat, and simmer
for about 30 minutes.
Add the sausage and cook for an additional
20 minutes.
Place the duck fat and pieces of duck in another
pan and cook until golden brown. Then remove
from the pan.
Add the lamb cubes to the pan and cook until
golden brown. Add the onions, garlic, and
tomatoes, pour in a little water and cook for
about 15 minutes.
Drain the beans and set aside. Chop the belly
pork and sausage. Discard the bouquet garni.
Pack the beans and all the pieces of meat into
preserving jars. Seal the jars, place in a large
saucepan of boiling water, and boil for about
1½ hours.
To serve the cassoulet, tip it into an ovenproof
dish, sprinkle with a layer of breadcrumbs and
heat it in the oven.
You can also add some grilled Toulouse sausages.

Cassoulet

Provençal-style Eggplant

Preparation time: 20 minutes
Cooking time: 1¼ hours
Makes 1 jar (1¾ pints)

2 tablespoons olive oil
2 garlic cloves, chopped
2 onions, chopped
1 bunch of parsley, chopped
10 ripe tomatoes, skinned
pinch of sugar
2 teaspoons herbes de Provence
2 eggplants, thickly sliced
2 bay leaves
salt

Sterilize the preserving jar in a large pan of boiling water for 10 minutes, then place upside down on a clean kitchen towel to drain.

Heat the olive oil in a large saucepan. Add the garlic, onions, parsley, tomatoes, sugar, and herbes de Provence, season with salt and cook over a low heat, stirring occasionally, for about 5 minutes, until the onions have softened.

Add the eggplant and bay leaves, then pour in sufficient water to half-fill the pan. Bring to a boil, then simmer for about 1¼ hours, until the vegetables have reduced.

Spoon the mixture into the jar, leaving 1–1½ inch headspace, then seal with an airtight lid.

Place the jar in a large pan, pour in water to cover, and bring to a boil. Boil for 1 hour, then leave the jar to cool in the water.

The following day, bring back to a boil for 30 minutes, then leave to cool.

Store the jars in a dark, dry place.

Provençal-style Eggplant

bottled vegetables

Peas and Carrots

Preparation time: 15 minutes
Cooking time: 1¼ hours

1½ cups peas, shelled
2 cups young carrots, cut into chunks
12 cups water
pinch of sugar
salt

Sterilize the preserving jars in a large saucepan of boiling water for 10 minutes, then remove the jars, and place upside down on a clean kitchen towel to drain.
Bring a large saucepan of lightly salted water to a boil. Add the peas and blanch for 3 minutes. Drain, rinse under cold running water, then drain again. Pack the peas into the jars and place the carrots on top.
Bring the measured water to a boil, add 2 teaspoons salt, and stir until dissolved.
Pour the salted water into the jars, leaving a 1–1½ inch headspace. Add the pinch of sugar.
Seal the jars with airtight lids. Place in a large saucepan, add water to cover, and bring to a boil. Boil for 1 hour, then leave to cool in the water in the saucepan.
Store in a dark, dry place.

Asparagus

Preparation time: 15 minutes
Cooking time: 1½ hours

1½ lb short asparagus spears of about equal thickness, peeled if necessary
12 cups water
salt

Sterilize the preserving jars in a large saucepan of boiling water for 10 minutes, then remove, and place upside down on a clean kitchen towel to drain.
Tie the asparagus spears in bunches of 10 using fine string. Bring a large saucepan of lightly salted water to a boil and add the asparagus bunches. Blanch for 3 minutes. Drain, rinse under cold running water, and drain again.
Untie the bundles and pack the asparagus into the jars, with the tips uppermost.
Bring the measured water to a boil, add 2 teaspoons salt, and stir until dissolved.
Pour the salted water into the jars to cover the asparagus, leaving a 1–1½ inch headspace at the top. Seal with airtight lids.
Place the jars in a large saucepan, add water to cover, and bring to a boil. Boil for 1 hour, then leave to cool in the saucepan of water.
Next day, bring back to a boil and boil for 30 minutes. Leave the jars to cool in the saucepan of water.
Remove when cool and store in a dark, dry place.

French Beans

Preparation time: 15 minutes
Cooking time: 1¼ hours

3½ cups French beans, trimmed
12 cups water
salt

Sterilize the preserving jars in a large saucepan of boiling water for 10 minutes, then remove, and place upside down on a clean kitchen towel to drain.
Bring a large saucepan of lightly salted water to a boil and add the beans. Blanch them for 3 minutes, then drain, and rinse under cold running water. Drain again and pack the beans in the jars.
Bring the measured water to a boil, add 2 teaspoons salt, and stir until dissolved.
Pour the salted water into the jars to cover the beans, leaving a 1–1½ inch headspace, and seal the jars with airtight lids.
Place the jars in a large saucepan, add water to cover, and bring to a boil. Boil for 1¼ hours, then leave the jars to cool in the water in the pan. Store in a dark, dry place.

Celery

Preparation time: 15 minutes
Cooking time: 1¼ hours

1½ lb celery, trimmed
12 cups water
salt

Sterilize the preserving jars in a large saucepan of boiling water for 10 minutes, then remove, and place upside down on a clean kitchen towel to drain.
Divide the celery into sections.
Bring a large saucepan of lightly salted water to a boil and add the celery. Blanch for 3 minutes, then drain, and rinse under cold running water. Drain again and pack into the jars.
Bring the measured water to a boil, add 2 teaspoons salt, and stir until dissolved.
Pour the salted water into the jars to cover the celery, leaving a 1–1½ inch headspace, and seal the jars with airtight lids.
Place the jars in a large saucepan, add water to cover, and bring to a boil. Boil for 1¼ hours, then leave the jars to cool in the water in the pan. Store in a dark, dry place.

French Beans

Swiss Chard

Preparation time: 15 minutes
Cooking time: 1¼ hours

6 cups Swiss chard, white stems only
12 cups water
salt

Sterilize the preserving jars in a large saucepan
of boiling water for 10 minutes, then remove,
and place upside down on a clean towel to drain.
Remove any stringy parts from the Swiss chard
and cut the stems into 1 inch lengths. Bring a
large saucepan of lightly salted water to a boil
and add the Swiss chard. Blanch for 3 minutes,
then drain, and rinse under cold running water.
Drain well again and pack into the jars.
Bring the measured water to a boil, add
2 teaspoons salt, and stir until dissolved.
Pour the salted water into the jars to cover
the Swiss chard, leaving a 1–1½ inch headspace,
and seal with airtight lids.
Place the jars in a large saucepan, add water to
cover, and bring to a boil. Boil for 1¼ hours, then
leave the jars to cool completely in the water in
the saucepan.
Store in a dark, dry place.

Tomato Coulis

Preparation time: 15 minutes
Cooking time: 2¼ hours

10 cups ripe beefsteak tomatoes, skinned,
quartered, and deseeded
6 tablespoons olive oil
3 garlic cloves, crushed
1 teaspoon sugar
1 small bay leaf
2 tablespoons fresh parsley, chopped
1 thyme sprig
4 basil leaves
salt and pepper

Sterilize the preserving jars in a large saucepan
of boiling water for 10 minutes, then remove,
and place upside down on a clean kitchen towel
to drain.
Cut the tomato quarters into large pieces.
Heat the olive oil in a deep pan, add the garlic,
and cook over a very low heat for 3 minutes.
Add the tomatoes, sugar, bay leaf, parsley, thyme,
and basil. Season with salt and pepper and stir
well. Cover and cook over a low heat for about
30 minutes.
Remove and discard the bay leaf and thyme.
Pour the tomato mixture into a food processor
or blender and process to a smooth purée.
Ladle the tomato coulis into the jars and seal
with airtight lids.
Place the jars in a large saucepan, add water
to cover, and bring to a boil. Boil for 1¼ hours.
Leave the jars to cool in the water in the pan.
Store in a dark, dry place.

TIP: This tomato coulis is a perfect garnish for
pizza, rice or meatballs.

Tomato Coulis

Tagliatelle with Mushrooms and Basil

Preparation time: 15 minutes
Cooking time: 20 minutes
4 servings

2 tablespoons olive oil, plus extra to serve
1 shallot, thinly sliced
1 cup Bottled Mushrooms
(see right), drained
3 cups dried tagliatelle
40 basil leaves, finely chopped
coarse sea salt and pepper

Heat the olive oil in a large frying pan, add the shallot, and cook over a low heat until golden. Add the mushrooms and cook for 2–3 minutes to release their flavor. Remove from the heat and keep warm.
Bring water to a boil in a 2-gallon saucepan. Add 3 tablespoons sea salt and the tagliatelle, bring back to a boil, and cook for 8–10 minutes, until tender but still firm to the bite. Drain and add to the frying pan. Return the frying pan to the heat and toss the mixture quickly, adding the chopped basil.
Serve with a little extra olive oil and pepper.

Bottled Mushrooms

Preparation time: 20 minutes + cooling
Cooking time: 1¼ hours

4–6 lb wild or mixed wild and
cultivated mushrooms
1 cup white wine
1 onion, cut into quarters
2–3 garlic cloves
bouquet garni, made from thyme, bay,
and savory
salt and pepper

Sterilize the preserving jars in a large saucepan of boiling water for 10 minutes, then remove, and place upside down on a clean kitchen towel to drain.
Cut any large mushrooms into halves or quarters. Blanch in a pan of boiling water for 2–3 minutes, then drain.
Pour 3 cups water into a large pan, add the wine, onion, garlic, and the bouquet garni and season with salt and plenty of pepper. Bring to a boil, add the mushrooms, and cook, stirring occasionally, for an additional 10 minutes.
Leave the mushrooms to cool in the cooking liquid, then remove with a slotted spoon, drain well, and pat dry. Strain the cooking liquid into a pitcher. Discard the contents of the strainer.
Pack the mushrooms into the jars. Pour the cooking liquid into the jars to cover the mushrooms, leaving a 1–1½ inch headspace and seal the jars with airtight lids.
Place the jars in a large saucepan, add water to cover, and bring to a boil. Boil for 1 hour, then leave the jars to cool in the water in the pan. Store in a dark, dry place.

Bottled Mushrooms

fruit
preserves

Strawberry Jam

**Preparation time: 10 minutes
+ overnight standing
Cooking time: 20 minutes
Makes 6 jars (8 oz each)**

4 cups strawberries, hulled
4 cups sugar
4 tablespoons lemon juice

Place all the ingredients in a dish, cover, and leave overnight in a cool place. The following day, prepare the jars according to the instructions at the bottom of the page.
Strain the strawberries, reserving the juice. Pour the juice into a preserving kettle. Bring to a boil, stirring constantly with a wooden spoon. Add the strawberries and boil for about 5 minutes. Strain the strawberries, return the sugary juice to the pan, and reduce over a medium heat for 5 minutes. Return the strawberries to the pan, bring back to a boil, and boil for 5 minutes.
Gently stir with the wooden spoon, then use a skimmer or slotted spoon to remove the scum that has formed on the surface.
Ladle the jam into the jars while still hot and seal according to the instructions at the bottom of the page.

Damson Jam

**Preparation time: 15 minutes
Cooking time: 20 minutes
Makes 6 jars (8 oz each)**

3 cups granulated sugar
½ cup water
4 cups damsons, halved and pitted
½ cup blanched almonds

Prepare the jars according to the instructions at the bottom of the page.
Put the sugar into a preserving kettle and pour in the water. Bring to a boil, stirring constantly, then add the damsons, and cook over a medium heat, stirring frequently, for about 20 minutes. Using a skimmer or slotted spoon, remove the scum that has formed on the surface. Stir in the almonds.
Ladle the jam into the jars while still hot and seal according to the instructions at the bottom of the page.

Apricot Jam

**Preparation time: 10 minutes
+ overnight standing
Cooking time: 20 minutes
Makes 4 jars (8 oz each)**

3½ cups ripe, firm apricots, cut in half and pitted
1½ cups sugar
2 tablespoons lemon juice

Place all the ingredients in a large dish, cover, and leave to stand overnight in a cool place. The following day, prepare the jars according to the instructions at the bottom of the page. Put the apricots, sugar, and lemon juice into a preserving kettle. Bring to a boil over a high heat, stirring constantly with a wooden spoon. Lower the heat to medium and cook for about 20 minutes. Stir with the wooden spoon, then use a skimmer or slotted spoon to remove the scum that has formed on the surface.
Ladle the jam into the jars while still hot and seal according to the instructions at the bottom of the page.

Raspberry Jam

**Preparation time: 10 minutes
Cooking time: 25 minutes
Makes 6 jars (8 oz each)**

4 cups raspberries
3 cups sugar
4 tablespoons lemon juice

Prepare the jars according to the instructions at the bottom of the page.
Put the raspberries, sugar and lemon juice into a preserving kettle, and bring to a boil over a fairly high heat, stirring constantly with a wooden spoon. Use a skimmer or slotted spoon to remove the scum that has formed on the surface.
Ladle the jam into the jars while still hot and seal according to the instructions at the bottom of the page.

Preparing the jars

Place the jars in a preheated oven, 225°F, for 5 minutes. Remove from the oven and leave to cool on a clean kitchen towel.

Potting the jam

Using a small ladle, fill the jars with jam to the top. Carefully wipe off any spills on the outside of the jars, then seal with airtight lids, and turn the jars upside down. Leave to cool, then store in a dark, dry place.

Rhubarb Jam

**Preparation time: 10 minutes
+ overnight standing
Cooking time: 20 minutes
Makes 7 jars (8 oz each)**

6 cups rhubarb, cut into short lengths
4½ cups sugar
1 unwaxed orange, sliced (optional)

Put the rhubarb and the sugar into a large dish,
cover, and leave to stand overnight in a cool
place. The following day, prepare the jars
according to the instructions at the bottom of the
page. Strain the rhubarb, reserving the juice, and
set aside. Pour the juice into a preserving kettle,
and bring to a boil over a high heat. Boil for 1–2
minutes, then add the rhubarb. Lower the heat
and simmer, stirring frequently with a wooden
spoon. Using a skimmer or slotted spoon, remove
the scum that has formed on the surface.
If you like, add the orange slices.
Ladle the jam into the jars while still hot and seal
according to the instructions at the bottom of
the page.

Plum Jam

**Preparation time: 10 minutes
+ overnight standing
Cooking time: 20 minutes
Makes 7 jars (8oz each)**

5 cups quetsch or other cooking plums,
halved and pitted
3 cups granulated sugar
4 tablespoons lemon juice

Put all the ingredients into a large dish, cover and
leave to stand overnight in a cool place.
The following day, prepare the jars according to
the instructions at the bottom of the page.
Put the plums, sugar, and lemon juice into a
preserving kettle, and bring to a boil over a high
heat, stirring constantly with a wooden spoon.
Remove the scum that has formed on the surface.
Ladle the jam into the jars while still hot and seal
according to the instructions at the bottom of
the page.

Seville Orange Marmalade

**Preparation time: 25 minutes
Cooking time: 1 hour
Makes 7 jars (8 oz each)**

15 unwaxed Seville oranges
4½ cups sugar
4 tablespoons lemon juice

Prepare the jars according to the instructions at
the bottom of the page.
Use a vegetable peeler to remove the rind from
3 of the oranges. Cut the rind into fine strips
about 1 inch long. Put the strips of rind into
a saucepan, add water to cover, and bring to
a boil. Lower the heat and simmer until the
rind feels tender to the touch.
Squeeze all the oranges. Put the orange juice,
sugar, and lemon juice into a preserving kettle,
and cook over a medium heat for about
40 minutes, stirring the liquid with a wooden
spoon. Add the orange rind, and cook for
about 20 minutes.
Using a skimmer or slotted spoon, remove the
scum that has formed on the surface.
Ladle the marmalade into the jars while still hot
and seal according to the instructions at the
bottom of the page.

Melon Jam

**Preparation time: 25 minutes + 2 hours standing
Cooking time: 50 minutes
Makes 6 jars (8 oz each)**

2 melons, halved, deseeded, peeled, and diced
2½ cups granulated sugar per 2 cups
of melon flesh
8 tablespoons lemon juice
a few blanched almonds

Prepare the jars according to the instructions at
the bottom of the page.
If the flesh from near the melon rinds seems hard,
blanch it in boiling water for 2 minutes.
Place the melon in a dish with the sugar and
lemon juice. Leave for 2 hours.
Pour the contents of the dish into a preserving
kettle and cook over a medium heat for about
50 minutes, stirring with a wooden spoon.
Using a skimmer or slotted spoon, remove the
scum that has formed on the surface.
Stir in the almonds.
Ladle the jam into the jars while still hot and seal
according to the instructions at the bottom of
the page.

Preparing the jars

Place the jars in a preheated oven, 225°F, for 5 minutes. Remove from the oven and leave to cool on
a clean kitchen towel.

Potting the jam

Using a small ladle, fill the jars with jam to the top. Carefully wipe off any spills on the outside of the jars,
then seal with airtight lids, and turn the jars upside down. Leave to cool, then store in a dark, dry place.

Mirabelle Plum Jam

**Preparation time: 10 minutes
+ overnight standing
Cooking time: 30 minutes
Makes 6 jars (8 oz each)**

4½ cups mirabelle or cherry plums
(or small plums), halved and pitted
3 cups fruit sugar
4 tablespoons lemon juice

Put all the ingredients into a large dish, cover,
and leave to stand overnight in a cool place.
The following day, prepare the jars according
to the instructions at the bottom of the page.
Put the plums, sugar, and lemon juice into a
preserving pan, and bring to a boil over a high
heat, stirring constantly with a wooden spoon.
Cook for about 30 minutes, then use a skimmer
or slotted spoon to remove the scum that has
formed on the surface.
Ladle the jam into the jars while still hot and seal
according to the instructions at the bottom of the
page.

Chestnut Jam

**Preparation time: 25 minutes
Cooking time: 35 minutes
Makes 6 jars (8 oz each)**

4 cups chestnuts
3 cups fruit sugar
1 vanilla pod

Prepare the jars according to the instructions at
the bottom of the page.
Cut into the chestnuts using a small, pointed
knife. Bring a large pan of water to a boil, add
the chestnuts, then drain. Remove both the shells
and their inner skins with the blade of a knife.
Bring another pan of water to a boil and add the
peeled chestnuts. Simmer gently for about
15 minutes, then remove the chestnuts from the
pan with a slotted spoon, and crush with the
back of a spoon. Alternatively push them through
a food mill.
Pour the chestnut cooking water into a preserving
kettle and add the sugar. Heat gently, stirring
continuously. As soon as the liquid starts to boil,
add the chestnuts and vanilla pod, and cook over
a medium heat, stirring frequently, for about
20 minutes.
Remove the vanilla pod.
Ladle the jam into the jars while still hot according
to the instructions at the bottom of the page.
Cut the vanilla pod into small pieces and add
a piece to each jar, then seal.

Preparing the jars

Place the jars in a preheated oven, 225°F, for 5 minutes. Remove from the oven and leave to cool on
a clean kitchen towel.

Potting the jam

Using a small ladle, fill the jars with jam to the top. Carefully wipe off any spills on the outside of the jars,
then seal with airtight lids, and turn the jars upside down. Leave to cool, then store in a dark, dry place.

Chestnut Jam

Blackcurrant Jelly

Preparation time: 20 minutes
Cooking time: 35 minutes
Makes 5–6 jars (8 oz each)

6 cups blackcurrants
½ cup water
4 cups sugar
4 tablespoons lemon juice

Prepare the jars according to the instructions at the bottom of the page.
Put the blackcurrants into a large, thick saucepan, pour in the water, and heat gently until the berries have burst. Place the fruit in a cheesecloth bag or wrap in a square of cheesecloth and squeeze hard over a large bowl to remove as much juice as possible. Discard the blackcurrant pulp.
Pour the juice into a preserving kettle and add the sugar and lemon juice. Cook over a medium heat for about 15 minutes.
Ladle the jelly into the jars while still hot and seal according to the instructions at the bottom of the page. Leave to cool, then store in a dark, dry place.

Redcurrant Jelly

Preparation time: 15 minutes
Cooking time: 15 minutes
Makes 5–6 jars (8 oz each)

6 cups redcurrants
4 cups sugar
4 tablespoons lemon juice

Prepare the jars according to the instructions at the bottom of the page.
Place the redcurrants in a cheesecloth bag or wrap in a square of cheesecloth and squeeze hard over a large bowl to remove as much juice as possible. Discard the redcurrant pulp.
Pour the juice into a preserving kettle and add the sugar and lemon juice. Cook over a medium heat for about 15 minutes.
Ladle into the jars and seal according to the instructions at the bottom of the page, then leave them to cool, and store in a dark, dry place.

TIP: You do not need to cook the redcurrants in advance, as you do for blackberries and blackcurrants. Redcurrant jelly sets very easily. In the past people even used to make redcurrant jelly with no cooking at all.

Preparing the jars

Place the jars in a preheated oven, 225°F, for 5 minutes. Remove from the oven and leave to cool on a clean kitchen towel.

Potting the jam

Using a small ladle, fill the jars with jam to the top. Carefully wipe off any spills on the outside of the jars, then seal with airtight lids, and turn the jars upside down. Leave to cool, then store in a dark, dry place.

Blackcurrant Jelly

White Wine Jelly

Preparation time: 25 minutes
Cooking time: 25 minutes
Makes 5 jars (8 oz each)

1 bottle medium dry white wine
2 cups apple juice
3 cups sugar

Prepare the jars according to the instructions at
the bottom of the page.

Pour the wine into a preserving kettle, and bring
to a boil. Remove from the heat and briefly
flambé the contents of the pan.

Pour in the apple juice and granulated sugar, stir
with a wooden spoon, and return to the heat.
Cook over a fairly high heat, stirring frequently,
for 15 minutes. Use a skimmer or slotted spoon
to remove the scum that has formed on the
surface.

Ladle the jelly into the jars while still hot and seal
according to the instructions at the bottom of the
page. Leave them to cool, then store them in a
dark, dry place.

TIP: This jelly is delicious with cold roast pork.

Preparing the jars

Place the jars in a preheated oven, 225°F, for 5 minutes. Remove from the oven and leave to cool on
a clean kitchen towel.

Potting the jam

Using a small ladle, fill the jars with jam to the top. Carefully wipe off any spills on the outside of the jars,
then seal with airtight lids, and turn the jars upside down. Leave to cool, then store in a dark, dry place.

White Wine Jelly

Apple and Quince Compote

**Preparation time: 15 minutes + cooling + chilling
Cooking time: 50 minutes**

2 ripe quinces, peeled, quartered, and cored
4 apples, peeled, quartered, and cored
½ cup fruit sugar
1 vanilla pod
½ cup water

Put all the ingredients into a large saucepan, bring to a boil, then cover, and simmer, stirring frequently, for about 50 minutes. If necessary, add a little more water to prevent the mixture from sticking to the bottom of the pan.
Leave the compote to cool, then chill in the refrigerator before serving.

TIP: Quinces are not widely available, but they are sometimes on sale in the late autumn. If you can't find them, use pears instead.

Spicy Pear Compote

**Preparation time: 15 minutes + cooling + chilling
Cooking time: 50 minutes**

6 cups pears, peeled, quartered, and cored
½ cup brown sugar
¼ teaspoon ground ginger
¼ teaspoon ground cinnamon
1 vanilla pod
½ cup water

Put all the ingredients into a large saucepan, bring to a boil, then cover, and simmer over a low heat for about 50 minutes.
Leave the compote to cool, then chill in the refrigerator. Serve with a little crème fraîche.

Compotes as preserves

To preserve compotes, reduce the cooking time for the fruit to 35 minutes. Prepare your jars as for jam. Ladle the hot compote into the jars, seal, and sterilize for 20 minutes in a large pan of boiling water. Leave them to cool before storing in a dark, dry place.

Spicy Pear Compote and Apple and Quince Compote

Crystallized Quince

Preparation time: 15 minutes + 3 days drying
Cooking time: 35 minutes

3½ cups ripe quinces, quartered
1 cup water
about 2 cups sugar
fruit sugar, for dusting

Put the quinces in a preserving kettle, add the water, and bring to a boil. Lower the heat and simmer for about 15 minutes, until tender.
Drain, peel and core then push the pieces of quince through a food mill on the finest setting. Alternatively, process to a purée in a blender or food processor.
Weigh the purée, then return it to the preserving kettle with the same weight of sugar, and bring to a boil. Simmer gently, stirring constantly, for 20 minutes, until the mixture forms a thick paste. Spoon the paste on to a cookie sheet lined with waxed paper and spread to an even depth of about 1 inch.
Leave to dry in a cool, dry place for 3 days, then stamp out shapes with a cookie cutter.
Dust the shapes with sugar and arrange them in an airtight container lined with a sheet of waxed paper.

TIP: Apples or pears can be used instead of quinces.

Crystallized Quince

Pears in Syrup

Preparation time: 15 minutes
Cooking time: 15 minutes

For each 1¾ pint jar:
7½ cups ripe, slightly firm pears, peeled, quartered, and cored
2 tablespoons fruit sugar
4 tablespoons lemon juice

Sterilize the preserving jars in a large pan of boiling water for 10 minutes, then place upside down on a clean kitchen towel to drain.
Pack the pears into the dry jars, sprinkle with sugar, and pour in the lemon juice.
Seal the jars with airtight lids and place in a large saucepan. Add water to cover, and bring to a boil. Boil for about 15 minutes.
Leave the jars to cool in the water, then store in a cool, dark place.

Wild Blackberries in Syrup

Preparation time: 15 minutes
Cooking time: 15 minutes

For each 1¾ pint jar:
4 cups wild blackberries
2 tablespoons fruit sugar
4 tablespoons lemon juice

Sterilize the preserving jars in a large pan of boiling water for 10 minutes, then place upside on a clean kitchen towel to drain dry.
Pack the blackberries into the dry jars, sprinkle with sugar, then pour in the lemon juice.
Seal the jars with airtight lids and place them in a large pan. Add water to cover, and bring to a boil. Boil for about 15 minutes.
Leave the jars to cool in the pan of water, then store in a cool, dark place.

TIP: Wild blackberries can be picked from July onwards. They are very succulent with a sharp, yet sweet flavour. Cultivated blackberries are almost as delicious, are widely available from all supermarkets, and may be substituted for wild.

Pears in Syrup

Plums in Syrup

Preparation time: 15 minutes
Cooking time: 15 minutes

For each 1¾ pint jar:
4 cups ripe, slightly firm plums
2 tablespoons fruit sugar
4 tablespoons lemon juice

Sterilize the preserving jars in a large pan of boiling water for 10 minutes, then place upside down on a clean kitchen towel to drain.
Pack the plums into the dry jars, then add the sugar and the lemon juice.
Seal the jars with airtight lids and place them in a large saucepan. Add water to cover and bring to a boil. Boil for about 15 minutes.
Leave the jars to cool in the water, then store them in a cool, dark place.

Cherries in Syrup

Preparation time: 15 minutes
Cooking time: 15 minutes

For each 1¾ pint jar:
4 cups ripe, slightly firm cherries
2 tablespoons fruit sugar
4 tablespoons lemon juice

Sterilize the preserving jars in a large pan of boiling water for 10 minutes, then place upside down on a clean kitchen towel to drain.
Pit 4 or 5 of the cherries, wrap the pits in the towel, and hit them with a hammer.
Pack the cherries into the dry jars, add the broken pieces of cherry pit and the sugar, and pour in the lemon juice.
Seal the jars with airtight lids and place them in a large saucepan. Add water to cover and bring to a boil. Boil for about 15 minutes.
Leave the jars to cool in the water, then store them in a cool, dark place.

Plums in Syrup

Vanilla Apricots

Preparation time: 15 minutes
Cooking time: 15 minutes

For each 1¾ pint jar:
3 cups ripe, slightly firm apricots,
halved and pitted, with 4–5 pits reserved
1 vanilla pod
2 tablespoons fruit sugar
4 tablespoons lemon juice

Sterilize the preserving jars in a large pan of
boiling water for 10 minutes, then place upside
down on a clean kitchen towel to drain.
Wrap the reserved apricot pits in the towel and
hit them with a hammer.
Pack the apricot halves into the dry jars with
the broken pieces of pit and the vanilla pod,
then add the sugar and lemon juice.
Seal the jars with airtight lids and place them in
a large saucepan. Add water to cover and bring
to a boil. Boil for about 15 minutes.
Leave the jars to cool in the water, then store
them in a cool, dark place.

Clementines in Syrup

Preparation time: 15 minutes
Cooking time: 1 hour

3 cups unwaxed clementines
1 cup fruit sugar
3 cups water

Sterilize the preserving jars in a large pan of
boiling water for 10 minutes, then place upside
down on a clean kitchen towel to drain.
Place the clementines in a saucepan of cold
water. Bring to a boil, then reduce the heat,
and simmer for about 12 minutes. Remove the
fruit and drain well.
Put the sugar into a heavy-based saucepan, pour
in the measured water and heat gently, stirring
until the sugar has dissolved. Bring to a boil,
then add the clementines, lower the heat, and
simmer for about 30 minutes.
Remove the pan from the heat and lift out the
oranges with a slotted spoon. Pack the
clementines into the jars and pour in the syrup.
Seal the jars with airtight lids and place them in
a large saucepan. Add water to cover and bring
to a boil. Boil for about 15 minutes.
Leave the jars to cool in the water, then store
them in a cool, dark place.

TIP: You will find that these clementines are
delicious with natural yoghurt. The syrup will
add a delicate flavour to fresh fruit salad.

Clementines in Syrup

Vanilla Sugar

Preparation time: 5 minutes
No cooking required

1 vanilla pod
4 cups fruit sugar

Slit the vanilla pod lengthwise using a small pointed knife. Scrape out the inside and remove and reserve the seeds.
Bury the vanilla pod in the sugar in a jar and stir in the seeds until evenly distributed.
Leave for 2–3 days before using.

TIP: This vanilla sugar is delicious in fruit salad. You can also use it to flavor cakes.

Star Anise Sugar

Preparation time: 5 minutes
No cooking required

2 star anise
4 cups fruit sugar

Add the star anise to the sugar in a jar and stir occasionally to mix.
Leave for 2–3 days before using.

TIP: This sugar is ideal for flavoring fruit salad. You can also make it with brown sugar (as illustrated opposite).

Cinnamon Sugar

Preparation time: 5 minutes
No cooking required

2 cinnamon sticks
4 cups soft brown sugar

Bury the cinnamon sticks in the brown sugar in a jar. Stir occasionally.
Leave for 2–3 days before using.

TIP: This cinnamon sugar is a delicious flavoring for hot chocolate, apple pies, and crumbles.

Star Anise Sugar and Vanilla Sugar

Cook's tips

Glazed Fruit Pie

This is a good way to give a professional touch to any fruit pie. Mix some fruit jelly, such as Redcurrant Jelly (see page 108) with a little water and a dash of liqueur, such as kirsch or amaretto, in a saucepan. Heat gently, stirring until the jelly has dissolved. Bake the pastry blind, then spread a thin layer of the mixture over the base. Arrange the fruit on top, then brush with the remainder of the jelly mixture. You will find that this greatly enhances both the flavor and appearance of your pie.

Chocolate Cupcakes with Clementines in Syrup

Grease 6 oven-proof custard cups with butter and lightly sprinkle with flour. Place 8 squares of chocolate and 1 cup diced butter in a heatproof bowl and melt over a pan of barely simmering water. Beat 8 egg yolks with 1 cup brown sugar until the mixture is pale and fluffy. Stir in the chocolate mixture. Beat 4 egg whites until stiff and fold into the mixture. Spoon the mixture into the custard cups so that they are about two-thirds full. Bake in a preheated oven, 300°F, for 30 minutes. About 5 minutes before the end of the cooking time, place sliced Clementines in Syrup (see page 120) on top of each custard cup. Serve warm.

Cheese and Crystallized Quince

Crystallized Quince (see page 114) can be eaten just as it is, but it is also great served with cheese.

Brioche and Damson Jam

As a treat for children, cut the tops off individual brioches, hollow them out slightly, and spread with a homemade preserve such as Damson Jam (see page 102).

Scones with Apricot Jam

The sweet, smooth taste of scones is even more delicious when combined with the tart flavor of Apricot Jam (see page 102). Remember to warm the scones in the oven for a few minutes before you serve them.

Linzertorte

Preparation time: 20 minutes
+ 1 hour resting + cooling
Cooking time: 30 minutes
4–6 servings

1 cup all-purpose flour
1 egg, lightly beaten
½ cup butter, diced (at room temperature)
1 cup fruit sugar
1 cup ground almonds
grated rind of ¼ unwaxed lemon
1 teaspoon ground cinnamon
1 teaspoon cocoa powder
½ cup Raspberry Jam (see page 102)
1 cup milk
salt

Sift the flour on to a work surface and make a
well in the centre. Put the egg, butter, sugar, and
a pinch of salt into the well. Mix lightly with your
fingertips, then add the almonds, lemon rind,
cinnamon, and cocoa powder. Gradually
incorporate the flour with your fingertips. Lightly
knead the dough, roll it into a ball, wrap in plastic
wrap, and leave to rest in the refrigerator for at
least 1 hour.
Roll out two-thirds of the dough and use to line
a 10-inch round or square pie dish. Spread the
jam evenly over the pastry base. Roll out the
remaining dough, and cut it into ½-inch wide
strips. Arrange these strips in a crisscross pattern
over the jam and brush with a little milk. Bake in
a preheated oven, 350°F, for 30 minutes. Leave to
cool before serving.

TIP: The torte is best served with whipped
cream. Your pastry will be even better if you
make it the day before.

Linzertorte

drying

Drying herbs is the best way to retain their aroma. You can use them throughout the year to prepare herbal teas as well as for cooking. This very simple technique is also useful for preserving medicinal herbs.

A word of advice

Herbs are best picked in the early morning and in dry weather. The ideal time is just after the dew has disappeared, but before the sun becomes hot, because the heat evaporates the plants' essential oils. Avoid harvesting in the rain.

Dry your herbs by spreading them out on a tray in a single layer without overlapping.

They are best stored in a dark, dry place. A jar in a cupboard or an airtight container will do.

Bay

Preparation time: 10 minutes + drying
No cooking required
Using pruning shears, carefully remove leaves from the tree. Do not use spotted or damaged leaves. Spread out the leaves in a dry place for a few days, turning them over occasionally, then store in an airtight container.

Thyme

Preparation time: 10 minutes + drying
No cooking required
Use pruning shears to cut some sprigs. Spread them out on a tray in a dry place and leave for a few days, turning them over occasionally. Then store in an airtight container.

TIP: A tea made from thyme is reputed to be excellent for colds—and in the kitchen it is a little marvel.

Rosemary

Preparation time: 10 minutes + drying
No cooking required
Remove several small branches using pruning shears. Spread them out on a tray in a dry place for a few days, turning them over occasionally, then store in an airtight container.

TIP: Rosemary is a very aromatic plant which subtly flavors meats and grilled fish. It is also widely used in Mediterranean recipes.

Rosemary

Lemon Verbena
Preparation time: 10 minutes + drying
No cooking required
Pick the verbena leaves. Spread them out on a tray and leave in a dry place, turning them over occasionally. Leave for about 2 weeks before using them to make tea. Verbena is said to be good for the digestion.
Store in an airtight container.

Cherry Stalks
Preparation time: 10 minutes + drying
No cooking required
Remove the stalks from freshly picked cherries. Spread them out on a tray in a dry place, turning them over occasionally. Leave for about 2 weeks before using them in tea.
This tea has diuretic properties.
Store in an airtight container.

Mallow
Preparation time: 10 minutes + drying
No cooking required
Collect some mallow flowers. Spread them out on a tray in a dry place, turning them over occasionally. Leave for about 2 weeks before using them in tisanes.
Store in an airtight container.

Orange Leaves
Preparation time: 10 minutes + drying
No cooking required
Collect some orange leaves. Spread them out on a tray in a dry place, turning them over occasionally. Leave for about 2 weeks before using them. Orange leaves are excellent for making a tea for drinking in the evening, as they have calming properties.
Store in an airtight container.

Camomile Flowers
Preparation time: 10 minutes + drying
No cooking required
Pick some camomile flowers, taking care to cut them off at the very ends of the stalks. Spread them out on a tray in a dry place, turning them over occasionally. Leave for about 2 weeks before using. Camomile tea is said to aid the digestion.
Store in an airtight container.

Linden Blossom
Preparation time: 10 minutes + drying
No cooking required
First pick the linden blossom—the trees are sometimes known as lime trees, although they are nothing to do with the citrus fruit trees. Spread out the flowers on a tray in a dry place, turning them over occasionally. Leave for about 2 weeks before using them.
Linden flower tea is reputed to have calming properties.
Store in an airtight container.

Dried Apples

Preparation time: 15 minutes
Cooking time: 6–9 hours

2 tablespoons lemon juice
6 cups apples, peeled, cored, and sliced
into rings

Half fill a bowl with cold water and stir in the lemon juice. Add the apple slices and set aside for 10 minutes.
Drain the slices and pat dry. Arrange them on a cookie sheet and place in a preheated oven on its lowest temperature setting for about 3 hours. Leave the oven door slightly ajar and occasionally turn the slices over.
Heat again for 3 hours the next day and a third time if necessary.
Store the fruit in an airtight container.

Dried Pears

Preparation time: 15 minutes
Cooking time: 6–9 hours

6 cups pears, peeled, halved, and cored

Pat the pears dry with paper towels and place on a cookie sheet. Place in a preheated oven on its lowest temperature setting for about 3 hours. Leave the oven door slightly ajar and turn the pear halves over occasionally.
Heat again for 3 hours the next day and a third time if necessary.
Store the fruit in an airtight container.

Dried Apricots

Preparation time: 15 minutes
Cooking time: 6–9 hours

6 cups apricots, halved and pitted

Arrange the apricot halves on a cookie sheet and place in a preheated oven at its lowest temperature setting for 3 hours. Leave the oven door slightly ajar and occasionally turn the apricots over.
Heat again for 3 hours the next day and a third time if necessary.
Store the fruit in an airtight container.

Dried Pears

Fruit and Chocolate Cookies

Dice small some Dried Pears, Dried Apples and Dried Apricots (see page 134). Use them instead of—or in addition to—more traditional fruit (like raisins and figs) and nuts (like almonds and hazelnuts) when decorating chocolate cookies.

Cherry-stalk Tea

Dried Cherry Stalks (see page 132) are renowned for their diuretic qualities, and are ideal for a little "detox." To prepare a tea, boil the stalks in water for 1 minute, then cover and leave to infuse.

Camomile Tea

Problems with your digestion? Try a good cup of tea made with dried Camomile Flowers (see page 132). The taste is bitter, but the effect is dramatic. You can also use an infusion of camomile as a mouthwash.

Lemon Verbena Ice Cream

You can make a delicious ice cream by
adding 5 tablespoons Lemon Verbena
Liqueur (see right) to custard into
which you have folded whipped
cream. Leave for at least 1 hour in the
freezer until set.

Lemon Verbena Liqueur

Put a handful of lemon verbena leaves
in a jar with 3 cups eau de vie
(colorless brandy), grappa or vodka.
Store in a cool, dark place for 40 days.
Filter the liquid and pour it into a
bottle. Put 1 cup granulated sugar
and ½ cup water into a saucepan.
Bring to a boil, stirring constantly,
then remove from the heat. Leave to
cool and when it becomes lukewarm,
add it to the bottle. Seal the bottle,
mix well, and store in a cool place.
Placing one 1–2 lemon verbena leaves
in the bottle will look attractive.

Apple Fromage Frais
Preparation time: 10 minutes
+ 30 minutes chilling
6 servings

4 cups fromage frais or curd cheese
2 cups Dried Apples (see page 134), diced
4 tablespoons clear honey

Place the fromage frais or curd cheese in a large
serving bowl. Add the diced apple and mix well.
Add the honey and stir well to mix. Chill in the
refrigerator for at least 30 minutes before serving.
Sprinkle with cinnamon to serve (optional).

TIPS: This dish could be served in tall glasses and
eaten with a long spoon.
Leave a small bowl of honey available, so that
people can sweeten it to their taste.

Apple Fromage Frais

syrups and
alcohol

Prunes in Alcohol

**Preparation time: 15 minutes
+ overnight soaking
No cooking required**

6 cups prunes
2 cups weak tea, cooled
1 cinnamon stick
½ cup fruit sugar
3 cups eau de vie (colorless brandy), grappa
or vodka

Put the prunes in a bowl, pour in the tea, and
leave to soak overnight.
Next day, sterilize a preserving jar in a large
saucepan of boiling water for 10 minutes.
Remove the jar and place upside down on a
clean kitchen towel to drain.
Drain the prunes and pack them into the dry jar.
Add the cinnamon stick and sprinkle in the sugar.
Pour in the eau de vie, grappa or vodka to cover
and seal the jar with an airtight lid.
Store in a cool, dark place for about 3 months
before opening.

Cherries in Alcohol

**Preparation time: 15 minutes
No cooking required**

4 cups ripe, slightly firm cherries,
stalks removed
1 cinnamon stick
½ cup fruit sugar
3 cups eau de vie (colorless brandy), grappa
or vodka

Sterilize a preserving jar in a large saucepan of
boiling water for 10 minutes. Remove and place
upside down on a clean kitchen towel to drain.
Pack the cherries into the dry jar. Add the
cinnamon stick and sprinkle in the sugar. Pour in
the eau de vie, grappa or vodka to cover and seal
the jar with an airtight lid.
Store in a cool, dark place for about 3 months
before consuming.

Prunes in Alcohol

Old Boy's Jam

**Preparation time: this "jam" is prepared over
several months from spring to autumn
Cooking time: 5 minutes**

good-quality fruits in season:
strawberries, hulled
apricots, halved and pitted
cherries, stalks removed
raspberries
peaches, pitted and quartered
grapes
plums, halved and pitted if large
pears, halved and cored.
1 cinnamon stick (optional)
fruit sugar
eau de vie (colorless brandy), grappa or vodka

Sterilize a large—at least 5 pint—preserving jar in
a large saucepan of boiling water for 10 minutes.
Remove and place upside down on a clean
kitchen towel to drain.
Place the first layer of fruit in the base of the dry
jar and add the cinnamon stick, if using.
To make the syrup put ½ cup sugar in a thick
saucepan. Pour in 2 cups water, and bring to
a boil, stirring constantly. Remove the pan from
the heat and leave to cool.
Pour the syrup over the fruits to cover, then add
1 cup eau de vie, grappa or vodka.
Seal the jar with an airtight lid and store in a
cool, dark place.
Continue making new layers of different fruits,
each time adding syrup to cover and eau de vie,
grappa or vodka. Re-seal with an airtight lid and
store in a cool, dark place.
When the jar is full, leave for about 3 months
before opening.

Old Boy's Jam

Lemon Syrup

Preparation time: 10 minutes + cooling
Cooking time: 15 minutes

4 cups fruit sugar
2 cups water
3 cups lemon juice
grated rind of 1 lemon

Put the sugar into a thick saucepan. Pour in the water and bring to a boil, stirring until the sugar has dissolved. Boil for 2–3 minutes, then remove the pan from the heat and set aside to cool. Pour the lemon juice into another thick pan and stir in the rind. Add the cooled syrup and heat gently for 5–10 minutes, stirring frequently. Leave to cool, then strain the liquid. Pour into a bottle and seal the top.

Blackcurrant Syrup

Preparation time: 15 minutes + cooling
Cooking time: 5 minutes

3 cups blackcurrant juice
3¾ cups fruit sugar

Pour the blackcurrant juice into a thick saucepan and add the sugar. Bring to a boil, stirring constantly until the sugar has dissolved. Boil for 2–3 minutes, then remove from the heat and leave to cool. Strain the syrup, pour into a bottle, and seal the top.

Mint Syrup

Preparation time: 15 minutes + cooling
Cooking time: 10 minutes

4 bunches of mint
3 cups water
4 cups fruit sugar

Place the mint leaves in a large bowl and pour in boiling water to cover. Cover with plastic wrap and leave to infuse overnight.
Next day, strain the liquid into a thick saucepan. Add the sugar and bring to a boil, stirring until the sugar has dissolved. Simmer for about 10 minutes, then remove the pan from the heat, and leave to cool. Pour into a bottle and seal the top

Syrups

Peach Wine

Preparation time: 10 minutes
+ 1 month macerating
No cooking required

2 handfuls of peach leaves
3 cups sweet white wine
1 cup eau de vie (colorless brandy), grappa
or vodka
½ cup fruit sugar

Place the peach leaves in a large jar. Add the wine, eau de vie, grappa or vodka, and the sugar. Cover and leave to macerate for about 1 month. Strain and bottle the wine.

TIP: Serve well chilled as an aperitif.

Walnut Wine

Preparation time: 10 minutes
+ 1 month macerating
No cooking required

6 fresh walnuts, shelled and quartered
3 cups sweet white wine
1 cup eau de vie (colorless brandy), grappa
or vodka
½ cup fruit sugar

Place the walnuts in a large jar. Add the wine, eau de vie, grappa or vodka, and sugar. Cover and leave to macerate for about 1 month, stirring occasionally. Strain and bottle the wine.

TIP: Serve well chilled as an aperitif.
Fresh walnuts, also known as wet walnuts, are available in the early autumn.

Orange Wine

Preparation time: 10 minutes
+ 8 days macerating
No cooking required

grated rind of 2 oranges
3 cups sweet white or rosé wine
¾ cup fruit sugar

Place the orange rind, sugar, and wine in a large bowl. Cover and leave to macerate for 8 days. Strain and bottle the wine.

Peach Wine and Walnut Wine

Cook's tips

Blackcurrant Kir

Pour a few drops of Blackcurrant
Syrup (see page 146) into a glass
before adding dry white wine.
Serve chilled as an aperitif.

Mint Granita

Fill a large glass with crushed ice and
pour a little Mint Syrup (see page 146)
over it. Stir and serve with a straw.

Lemon Sherbet with Syrup

A last minute tip: just as you serve a
sherbet, sprinkle it with a few drops
of Lemon Syrup (see page 146).

Peach and Orange Spiced Fruit Salad

Pour 1 cup Peach Wine (see page 148)
into a pan. Add the juice of 1 orange
and a cinnamon stick and bring to a
boil. Remove from the heat and leave
to cool.
Spoon the mixture over fruit salad and
serve well chilled.

Cherry and Rosemary Clafoutis

**Preparation time: 20 minutes
+ 20 minutes standing
Cooking time: 30 minutes
4 servings**

½ cup white or brown sugar
1 egg yolk
2 eggs
1½ tablespoons all-purpose flour, sifted
2 tablespoons ground almonds
1 cup milk
½ cup light cream
1 cup Cherries in Alcohol (see page 142)
1 rosemary sprig
salt

Whisk together the sugar and egg yolk in a bowl, then whisk in the whole eggs. Fold in the flour, almonds, and a pinch of salt and whisk well. Stir in the milk and cream, then set aside in a cool place to rest for 10 minutes. Meanwhile, arrange the cherries and rosemary in a well-greased ovenproof dish. Whisk the batter again, pour it over the fruit and cook in a preheated oven, 350°F, for 30 minutes. Leave to stand for about 10 minutes and serve slightly warm.

Cherry and Rosemary Clafoutis

Old Boy's Fresh Fruit Salad

Preparation time: 15 minutes + 3 hours chilling
No cooking required

2 oranges, peeled and cut into chunks
2 apples, cored and diced
1 banana, peeled and sliced
1 kiwifruit, peeled and sliced
1 small pineapple, peeled, and chopped
1 small mango, peeled, pitted, and diced
a few mint leaves
2 tablespoons raw sugar
1 cup liquor from Old Boy's Jam (see page 144)
mint sprigs, to decorate

Place the pieces of fruit in a large bowl, sprinkle
the sugar over it, pour on the liquor, and mix
gently. Cover with plastic wrap and chill for at
least 3 hours.
Decorate with mint sprigs and serve well chilled.

TIP: You can add some fruits in alcohol to the
fresh fruits, if you wish.

Old Boy's Fresh Fruit Salad

Appendices

Table of Recipes

With thanks to

- *Pasta Luna*, 15 rue Mézières, 75006 Paris, France
- "Airelle" and "Miss Olive"
- Gérard Ciprès for the creation of certain recipes,
including the awesome *Cherry and Rosemary Clafoutis*

Bravo to Akiko!

First published by Marabout, an imprint of Hachette-Livre
43 Quai de Grenelle, Paris 75905, Cedex 15, France
© 2002 Marabout (Hachette-Livre)
© Les recettes d'Amandine (text)
© Akiko Ida (photographs)
Under the title *Les Recettes d'Amandine, Conserves Maison*
All rights reserved

English language translation produced by Translate-A-Book, Oxford

English Translation © 2004, Octopus Publishing Group Ltd, London
This edition published by Hachette Illustrated UK, Octopus Publishing Group,
2–4 Heron Quays, London, E14 4JP

Proof-reading (French edition) Philippe Rollet
Editing: Chrystel Arnould

ISBN: 1-84430-079-X
Printed by Tien Wah, Singapore